Co

CATEGORIES

Beaches

ROUND ISLAND PRESERVE

Blustery 20-knot winds rolled in the March day I visited this *5-acre preserve.* It was still fun 'cause you can nuzzle your buggy up to the tree line to watch and marvel at crashing waves. In GOOD WEATHER folks toast and roast (both hot dogs and bodies) on 1000 feet of beach! A few sheltered tables perch where dunes mingle with pines at this SECLUDED PARK!!

ORCHID ISLAND FL   INDIAN RIVER COUNTY   NEAR VERO BEACH
OPEN DAILY 8-SUNSET   FREE

JAYCEE AND GOVERNMENT TRACKING STATION BEACH

It will handle the CROWDS. Plenty of parking for 300 cars. A L-O-O-O-NG BOARDWALK *parallels duneline* so you can ogle beachside "goings on", yet, still have dry tootsies. Bathers will find a NARROW BEACH, sheltered picnic sites, a wee tot playground and grassy area. Life-guards are present and when you see the *satellite dishes* hovering over the Atlantic you'll know why they call the site GOVERNMENT TRACKING STATION!!!

VERO BEACH FL   NORTH OF RD. 60 ON A1A
OPEN DAILY 8AM-SUNSET   FREE

WABASSO BEACH PARK...A GOOD WEEKDAY BEACH

This is an *easy beach* to reach JUST NORTH of SR 510 and A1A on ORCHID ISLAND. There's access at Cayman or Sandpiper Roads, Sand Dollar Lane and Pebble Path. It's a *developed* beach with lifeguards, showers and restrooms. FUNSIES include fishing, swimming and picnicking *plus* there are boating facilities. Wabasso is crowded *on weekends,* folks, so if you can go *during the week,* that's your best bet. *Parking is street-side...*another reason to avoid the weekend!!!

DIRECTIONS ABOVE   OPEN DAILY   FREE

FREDRICK DOUGLAS OCEAN PARK

Pink oleanders and green seagrape trees usher you along the shell-paved road to a long beach where you can simply sit in the car to watch bathers and frothy waves roll over one another. Palms and Aussy pines shade tables, restrooms and grills. HIGH TIDE gobbles up a good chunk of sands so that your swimming beach is only about 200 feet wide — but still plenty room for frolicking. THE DRIVE to F. Douglas is relaxing because *several scenic green coves and small bays* keep popping up on the INTRACOASTAL SIDE of Road A1A!!

HUTCHINSON ISLAND, FL 3 MI. SOUTH OF FT. PIERCE
ON RD. A1A   OPEN DAILY   FREE

RICHARD KREUSLER BEACH

Lots of HUB-HUB here aside from people bumping and bouncing in the surf. A long BOARDWALK, small shops with striped awnings and choices of INDOOR or OUTSIDE EATERIES add pizzas to this beach. There are chickee huts, cabana and float rentals and always the PASSING PARADE of *latest beach styles!!!* Parking is METERED, but you may also use CITY BUS SERVICE to go surf splashing!!!

LAKE WORTH FL NEAR JUNCTURE RD. 802 AND HWY. A1A
OPEN DAILY 8 AM-SUNSET   FREE

PHIPPS OCEAN PARK

Special care was taken to preserve THE DUNES (some being 20 or 30 feet high). This EXTENSIVE PARK occupies about 1000 feet of Atlantic oceanfront. Perched on the duneline are *banyans and gumbo limbo giants* shading lunch tables and grills. Approach to the swim area is up-n-over the dunes. Atop the dunes is a pretty walkway affording "squirrel encounters" and ocean vistas!! Parking is METERED and Phipps can accommodate the CROWDS.

LAKE WORTH FL 2 MI. NORTH OF RD. 802 ON HWY. A1A
OPEN DAILY   FREE

FORT LAUDERDALE SANDS

Blustery days deposit sand on the bustling multi-lane highway which runs beside the beach. Almost 3 MILES OF OCEANFRONT are for *public use.* A green picnic park area huddles on the south stretch. Appetites have lots of choices at *block after block* of 'DOG AND GROG" diners and delis across the street. If your greenbacks hold out, ANY TYPE OF FLOATING DEVICE can be rented. Traffic and parking can be bothersome, but I liked the ACTION-PACKED AREA!! (Always something to gander at!) Check out the PEDESTRIAN TUNNEL under A1A (north beachside). It leads to HUGH TAYLOR BIRCH, 180-acre state park! V-E-R-Y S-P-E-C-I-A-L.

FT. LAUDERDALE FL SUNRISE BLVD. ON HWY. A1A
OPEN DAILY 8 AM-SUNSET   FREE

LAKE WORTH BEACH

Take time to get some *sand in your shoes!* LAKE WORTH BEACH is the perfect spot. A beautiful stretch of sandy beach ruffled with Atlantic SURF plus POOL for *still-water swimmers.* There's a 1300-foot FISHING PIER where you can dangle a hook, as well as a PICNIC AREA with GRILLS to satisfy the "hungries". Play GOLF at the BEACH? *You bet!* Shuffleboard, too — and even a CASINO. It's all here under the sun. Lifeguards are on duty and there are showers and restrooms for your convenience. Parking is available or you can take advantage of public transportation.

PALM BEACH FL ON SR A1A (OCEAN BLVD.)
OPEN DAILY   FREE

VERO SWIM BEACH — A VILLAGE ATMOSPHERE

As you buzz south on A1A, you'll come to the junction of Rd. 60. And

THAT, friends, means you've reached VERO SWIM BEACH!! Access is via TWO steep walks and some 20 steps down to the beach itself. In addition to SWIMMING and PICNICKING you'll enjoy the 20 or so neat LITTLE SHOPS clustered around LITTLE SQUARE *which gives this beach its village atmosphere!* Kinda different!! Lifeguards are on duty here and there's free parking for about 200 cars.

DIRECTIONS ABOVE VERO BEACH FL
OPEN DAILY   FREE

SOUTH BEACH PARK...GRASS GROWS ALL AROUND

Green grass at the BEACH? Yup! *Green grass, white sand and curling waves* along *300-feet* of *developed beachfront make SOUTH BEACH PARK one dee-lightful spot!! Add to this PAVILIONS where you can grill your favorite EATS to stifle the "hungries", showers and comfort stations, plus a BIRD WALK and three DUNE OVERWALKS — well, it's a neat beach get-away!* Not so much *hub-bub* as some beaches. There are lifeguards on duty plus free parking for about 300 cars with more parking across the street. Take A1A east, go left on Causeway Blvd. to Ocean Drive and you're there!!

DIRECTIONS ABOVE VERO BEACH FL
OPEN DAILY   FREE

JUPITER TO JUNO SANDS — AS FAR AS THE EYE CAN SEE

What a stretch ! South of Jupiter Inlet, There are 3.2 MILES of public-access beach starting at CARLIN PARK. There are *pull-offs* where you can park and watch the gorgeous GREEN WATERS of the Atlantic *beyond the dunes and sea grapes.* BOARDWALKS *lead down to the beach* at intervals over this 3-mile stretch. CARLIN PARK is 126 ACRES BIG with parking for about 500 cars. There are *sheltered picnic tables on top of the dunes,* a CIVIC CENTER and the PARK GALLEY SNACK BAR. There is even a *little baseball park* here! Also a bit of HISTORY in the shape of a SHIP'S WHEEL from the Spanish Schooner *AVANDE,* wrecked off the Keys *around 1900.* JUNO BEACH PARK has *everything* from PLAY-GROUNDS to SNACK BARS — even FISHING!!! It's located half-way along this drive on the WEST SIDE of A1A. The last mile is a BIKE AND JOG TRAIL on the *ocean side of the roadway.*

SOUTH A1A JUPITER TO JUNO FL
OPEN DAILY   FREE

DELRAY BEACH — 7000 FEET OF PURE BEACH SAND

Ooohh! It's a WINNER!!! JUST BEAUTIFUL! *All along the drive* on the Atlantic side, there's NOTHING to obstruct access to the ocean for about THREE MILES! There are coconut palms here, METERED PARKING (PLENTY of room for the parkers), lifeguards on duty, CABANAS — *you can rent 'em* — and small OCEAN SAILBOATS for rent if that's your thing. Across the road are some OUTDOOR EATERIES where you can *quaff goodies.* At ATLANTIC AVE. (806) is a CULTURAL PAVILION and there are benches where you can *overlook the ocean.* All along the beachside are beautiful SILVER EUCALYPTUS TREES...soooo pretty !!!

A1A DELRAY BEACH FL
OPEN DAILY   FREE

CASINO BEACH PARK — LOTS TO DO HERE

Ever hear of HYPOLUXO? Betcha haven't! That was the *original name* of the City of LAKE WORTH!! It was renamed in 1913 after LAKE Worth — which got ITS name from *Gen. William J. Worth* whose strategy ended the GREAT SEMINOLE WARS! So much for history! As you drive along A1A in Lake Worth, you'll come to R802 (LAKE AVE.). Hang a left here and drive to where the road dead-ends. Here is RICHARD G. KREUSLER PARK and just down the line is CASINO BEACH PARK — also known as LAKE WORTH BEACH AND FISH PIER. At the Kreusler Park end, go up a big sand dune — almost 30 feet high — and there it is: a BIG beach park. There's METERED PARKING for about a thousand cars. There are BRICK PROMENADES, *lifeguards, showers and restrooms,* SHADED TABLES and a NICE BEACH with little CHICKEE UMBRELLAS at intervals. At Lake Worth Beach you have the 1300-foot FISH PIER which is *lit at night.* There are a couple of SHADED STOPS — one-half way out, the other at the end. I'm not sure what folks were catchin', but *they were sure haulin' 'em in!!* Check local knowledge for what's biting. Lake Worth Municipal CASINO has LOTS of SHOPS *where you can spend that good ole* GREEN, and for those who don't enjoy the surf, take a dip in the big MUNICIPAL SWIMMING POOL! There's also a PICNIC AREA with grills, a GOLF COURSE and a SHUFFLEBOARD COURT here.

DIRECTIONS ABOVE LAKE WORTH FL
OPEN DAILY   PARKING FEE

RED REEF PARK
WHERE THE BAREFOOT MAILMAN WALKED

PARKS around here are WOWSERS! Like its sister park up the line, Red Reef *strrretches all the way from the Atlantic to the ICW!!* There's a PUBLIC GOLF COURSE — can you believe it? — on the side of a 30-FOOT SAND DUNE! Parking here for about a THOUSAND cars...nice LONG beaches with an OCEAN BOARDWALK, a PAVILION, GRILLS, PICNIC TABLES, BEACH SHOWERS and restrooms. *Life-guards are on duty up and down the beach.* The ICW PART of the park is like a DEEP RAIN FOREST with 40-FOOT SEA GRAPES, MANGROVES — *all kinds of tropical growth!! A real pretty place to TARRY!!! ENJOY!*

1400 N. OCEAN BLVD. (A1A)
BOCA RATON, FL — (561) 393-7810   OPEN DAILY

BLOWING ROCKS — BRING YOUR SNORKELING GEAR

Talk about SCENIC!! This one is a PRIZE!!! You have 600 feet of DEVELOPED SANDY BEACH...ROCK FORMATIONS...CLIFFS and a CORAL REEF!!! Things to DO? Read on! *Fishing, surfing, snorkeling, swimming,* of course, and a SHELL HUNTER's PARADISE! There's a NATURE TRAIL, showers and comfort stations with *facilities for the handicapped.* Lifeguards are on duty here WEEKENDS and HOLIDAYS. *There are no food concessions,* so bring the NECESSARIES! FREE PARKING! Blowing Rocks Beach is located in CORAL COVE PARK at A1A and R707, one mile south of Martin County on Jupiter Island.

DIRECTIONS ABOVE   OPEN DAILY
JUPITER ISLAND FL (561) 747-3113   ADMISSION

POMPANO SWIM BEACH — GORGEOUS GOLDEN SAND

One block south of A1A and just a STONE'S THROW from Pompano Fish Pier, is POMPANO PUBLIC BEACH — and I mean *there's a lotta beach here!!!* About 2000 feet LONG and 3-400 feet WIDE — *plenty of room to spread out!* There are CABANA RENTALS if you like, life-guards on duty 9 a.m.-5 p.m....and all the NECESSARIES for a day at the beach: *picnic shelters* and *tables, grills,* a CHILDREN'S PLAYGROUND, plus showers and restrooms. All along the beach SQUARES of *shops and restaurants!* You can do a little shopping, eat our and STILL CATCH THOSE RAYS!!! If you tire of surfing and sunbathing, *walk a couple of blocks east* and see the FISHING FLEET or watch the DRAW-BRIDGE flop up and down!! There are a number of nice small MOTELS here — moderately priced. This is one of the FEW *southern beach areas* where these accommodations can still be found instead of a solid concrete wall of condos!!

POMPANO BEACH BL   OPEN DAILY
POMPANO BEACH FL   FREE

BOCA'S SOUTH BEACH...A WHOPPING BEACH

Going to the beach is EASY in Boca! There are *so many beach parks* here!! South Beach Park has 2700 feet of OCEAN FRONTAGE — plenty of room to find YOUR SPOT IN THE SUN!! Located EAST of A1A, it has a UNIQUE FEATURE: ELEVATED WALKWAYS which *span the dunes!!!* There are asphalt walkways, too, beach showers, restrooms and *professional lifeguards* on duty from 9 a.m. to 5 p.m. Parking for 230 cars and two entrances.

BOCA RATON, FL N. OCEAN BLVD. (561) 393-7810   OPEN DAILY

WABASSO SAND SHORES   3 CHOICES

Newest natural gem is TREASURE SHORES PARK.Its *66 acres* fronts on glittering Atlantic Ocean. Life guards a-plenty, clean bathhouses, a kiddie playground, lots of carparks and 3,715 feet of SWIM BEACH!!! GOLDEN SANDS PARK covers *14 acres* with 1,040 feet of foamy shores for bathing... lastly is weensie AMBER SAND BEACH where one dune "crossover" leads to over 3,000 feet of green wave sand...If you think Wabasso is a "curious" name, you're right. In 1898 settlers from OSSABAW, Ga. spelled the name of their Georgia hometown backwards - Thank the stars they didn't stick with OSS-A-BAW!!!

WABASSO FL NORTH OF TOWN HWY A1A   OPEN DAILY   FREE

Boating & Canoeing

LOXAHATCHEE RIVER CANOE TRAIL

What a way to go! *Gliding along the beautiful LOXAHATCHEE RIVER — the ONLY wild, natural river in southeast Florida —* 17 whole miles of it! *Super scenic* with cypress trees, fern-draped banks, deer, raccoons and birds, birds, birds! Anhinga, osprey, bald eagles, great blue heron and more. The Trail begins at the State Road 706 bridge and ends at JONATHAN DICKINSON STATE PARK north of West Palm Beach on Highway A1A. *Bring the necessaries* for this one-day trek by water. *Inexperienced canoers should beware the hazards of shallow water, logs and deadfalls* — and NO ONE should attempt this trip in extremely DRY WEATHER. Otherwise, enjoy!!!

JUPITER FL   OPEN DAILY   BOAT RENTAL (561) 746-1466
ON SR 706, 1¼ MILE W OF JUPITER INTERCHANGE   PARK (772) 546-2771

PELICAN ISLAND — A NATIONAL "FIRST"

An HISTORIC ISLAND lies not far from marker 70 in the *Indian River:* PELICAN ISLAND NATIONAL WILDLIFE REFUGE. *The very first national wildlife refuge in the NATION!!!* Established in 1903 at the direction of *PRESIDENT TEDDY ROOSEVELT, the island is a major nesting site* for the *endearing* and ENDANGERED BROWN PELICAN. If you have access to a shallow-draft boat or canoe, you can FISH around the *island's shores,* take *pictures* of ALL the birds (not just Brownies) and bird-watch to your heart's content! BUT DON't GO ASHORE!!! *This island IS strictly for the birds!!*

VISITOR CENTER (ORCHID ISLAND) HWY A1A-N. OF RD 510
MARKER 70, ICW   ACCESS DAWN TO DUSK BY BOAT
SEBASTIAN FL   FREE

SEBASTIAN RIVER CANOEING — A SCENIC PADDLE

Paddle YOUR OWN CANOE or *rent one in Grant!!* Here's your chance for a *nice relaxing trip down this pretty river!* It's a 7-mile stretch, some of it WILD...with HIGH BANKS, SAND BARS here and there and *tucked back among the trees,* SETTLERS' HOMES! *Verrrry rustic!!!* This is an EASY PADDLE downstream. The put-in is on Highway 512 in Sebastian. A GREAT GETAWAY!!

DIRECTIONS ABOVE   OPEN DAILY
SEBASTIAN FL   FREE

SOUTH INLET PARK — SMALL BUT NICE

This is a COUNTY park just south of BOCA INLET. You can see the BOATS coming and going here! There's a *parking and pier jetty* with space for 81 cars (3 handicapped) and boy, you park in LUXURY in the shade of a GUMBO LIMBO TREE !!! You can FISH from the jetties — there were a number of fisherfolk the day I was there. *Spread your picnic lunch* on tables shaded by AUSSIE PINES on the beach — and *barbecue* your hot dogs, hamburgers or whatever on the handy GRILLS. There's a PAVILION where you can watch the DRAWBRIDGE do its thing as boats come and go through the inlet. There are restrooms and lifeguards are on duty from 7 a.m. to 5:30 p.m.

S. OCEAN BLVD.   OPEN DAILY
BOCA RATON, FL (561) 393-7810   ADMISSION

KISSIMMEE VALLEY RIVER BASIN

56 miles of canals plus 47 miles of meanderings through a CHAIN OF

11 LAKES makes KISSIMMEE (mulberries yonder) a top spot for outdoor fun. MULBERRIES YONDER RIVER has kept a *primitive character* 'cause the boys with the big yachts and "rooster tails" gotta stay home (there are 7 locks and 7 bridges...11 1/2 ft. clearance). A 10-mile project (east of Sebring) is restoring the river to historic OXBOWS and natural MARSHES!! Choices are many for exploring "the wilds". KISSIMMEE STATE PARK boasts 5030 acres with full marina, and 13 miles of hiking backtrails. I spotted the red-billed SANDHILL CRANES nearby and stood in awe of the "live oak forest". Deer herds are healthy in the river basin, numbering about 500. Southeast of Lake Kissimmee is an outstanding "wilderness", PRAIRIE-LAKES PRESERVE. It is 8000 acres of "green" (wet and dry). I enjoyed booting part of a 12.5-mile path beside a running stream shaded by tall forest giants!! South Loop will lead to 43,282 acres of THREE LAKES WILDLIFE AREA (for the hale and hearty!). BRAHMAN ISLAND in south Lake K. is a breeding farm for large exotic animals...no peeking — it's private... If you're looking for *someplace different* away from the maddening crowd, K.V.R.B. is IT!!! Get Kissimmee Waterway Map. South Florida Water Management District, P.O. Box V-33, Old Gun Club Rd., West Palm Beach, FL 33402. Call (407) 686-8800 or 1-800-432-2045. *Campers with boats* will go bananas over OKEE-TANTIE Rec Park. I spent a week at OKEE where MULBERRIES YONDER RIVER flows into the great LAKE OKEECHOBEE. Info (863) 763-2622.

OKEECHOBEE FL (SOUTH END) OR KISSIMMEE FL (NORTH END)
OPEN DAILY   FREE

Cities Florida Style

GRANT & MICCO — THE FISHING TWINS

Drive down Rt. 1, south of Palm Bay, to the sleepy old towns of GRANT and MICCO. Just a hoot and a holler under 4 miles apart, these friendly communities have the *Indian River* at their doorsteps — I mean they *snuggle* right up to it — and FISHING is the *biggest game in town?* Save the "hungries" till you get here, folks, 'cause they not only *catch'em* they *serve'*em!!! All kinds of SEAFOOD RESTAURANTS abound in both towns, offering fresh local *fruits of the sea.* For two days in February, GRANT comes alive as THOUSANDS flock from *near and far* to the ANNUAL SEAFOOD FESTIVAL...one of Florida's *finest!* Old family recipes are trotted out and served up in a variety of *yummy seafood dishes!* In MICCO, with its *cedar trees,* the fellas in the FIRE DEPT. are *equally famous* for their PANCAKE BREAKFASTS served at various times throughout the year. And along with the *delectables* is the VIEW!! *Serene, lovely spoil islands* dot the river, *pelicans soar* and *dolphins play.* Spend some time in these laid-back old towns which have (somehow) *avoided the modern hustle* for the lifestyle of yesteryear.

US 1, GRANT & MICCO FL   OPEN DAILY   FREE

SEBASTIAN — "5046 FRIENDLY PEOPLE & 6 OLD GROUCHES" —

So says the *Welcome sign* as you drive into this old Florida city. And it's here you'll find one of the *prettiest drives* around. Cut off Rt. 1 onto INDIAN RIVER ROAD — it's only about 4 miles long, *but well worth the detour.* You'll see several 2 and 3 story homes all beautifully restored, *standing amid oak groves.* In the river, *commercial fisherfolk* in their TRADITIONAL WHITE BOOTS ply their trade. Park the car and stroll along the drive from which you can see the *islands in the river* with their ever-present *bird life.* Explore the *little green parks* tucked here and there — it's a good chance to S-T-R-E-T-C-H your legs a bit. Chow time??? This is THE PLACE for *seafood* — all fresh and *yum-yum good!!!!* Maybe you'd like to go fishing aboard a commercial charter fishing vessel — *the fleet's right here!!* Or pause at the Sebastian Yacht Club to admire their fleet — all under 30 feet! It's a nice change of pace!

DIRECTIONS ABOVE   OPEN DAILY
SEBASTIAN FL   FREE

BOCA RATON — A DREAM COME TRUE

You HAVE to SEE it, *this dream city!!!* Boca is YOUNG as cities go...most of it new...and for my money, the MOST BEAUTIFUL CITY IN FLORIDA!!! It's a PLANNED city and *it shows.* Everything is *so tastefully done* — even the WATER TOWER is a *work of art!* The landscaping is STUN-NING ...FLORAL ARTISTRY! The HOMES are just gorgeous but so are the business buildings! In fact, *there's a mix of residences and businesses here so beautifully done* that it's hard to tell one from the other!! Incredible!! There's GREEN everywhere...lovely PARKS, WATER-VIEWS, BEACHES!!! Addison Misner started it — *this* was his DREAM — *others have brought it to fruition* and the result is a MAGNIFICENT ARCHITECTURAL MOSAIC! *Don't miss this.* It's an EXPERIENCE!

BOCA RATON FL   OPEN DAILY   FREE

PORT SALERNO — WHERE THE BOATERS GO

Don your skipper's hat, this is BOAT COUNTRY!!! There are literally THOUSANDS of 'em docked or anchored in *picturesque* MANATEE POCKET here in Port Salerno! Every size, every description, probably every MAKE! As you wander along the piers here, take a look at some of the BOAT NAMES. I saw some good ones: A handsome 90-footer called *POOPSIE,* another named *HELEN HIGHWATER (think about that one!)* and a big beauty called *HERMAN'S ERMINE!!! Very popular* is PIRATE'S COVE MARINA & RESTAURANT on Bayview Ave. The restaurant is a 3-story wood INN OF YORE and its KITCHEN plays to a FULL HOUSE *every night!* Port Salerno is home to the *local commercial* FISHING FLEET and I saw many *shore-side* FISHERFOLK in their *traditional white boots.* This is a charming, unspoiled community — *a rarity anymore!* Seafood restaurants abound here! — And you can rent a boat to visit ST. LUCIE INLET STATE PARK, *accessible only by boat.*

A1A PORT SALERNO, FL   OPEN DAILY
                                                          FREE

DAVIE — RODEO CITY

52 RODEOS per year provide galloping entertainment! Davie sports a

western theme (lots of ranches plus 7 stores overflowing with boots, buckles, cowpoke sombreros...and HAY...). RESIDENTIAL realtors advertise: *"4 horses to 1 square acre."* While it is an equestrian town, there is a unique OPEN SPACE PROGRAM — making Davie *"An Oasis of Green in a Sea of Concrete"!!* Davie's other half, COOPER CITY, has been named "Tree City, USA". A covered rodeo pavilion seats 5000 with standout WEEKLY RODEOS. November and March are championship affairs drawing world-wide competitors. Don't blink an eye if you see horses on the streets or hitched in parking lots!!! Take in NOVA University and BUEHLER PLANETARIUM (good excuse for hanging around this refreshing town)...don't forget APPLES...for you know who!!!

Davie Cooper City, FL 10 miles SW of Ft. Lauderdale
Bergeron Rodeo Ground, 4271 Davie Rd.   (954) 384-7075

LAUDERDALE-BY-THE-SEA — A SPECIAL PLACE

It's so TINY — this SEASIDE COMMUNITY on Florida's GOLD COAST! Nestled between the Atlantic and the ICW, *it's not much more than 1 1/2 miles long and maybe half a mile wide!* NO HIGH RISES HERE!!! Just neat, *attractive homes and businesses, shops and restaurants.* Lots of those!! And all with a flavor of YESTERYEAR. Capping it all, is one GORGEOUS BEACH!!! *Beautiful golden sand* all spic'n span (it's *cleaned daily!.)* Lauderdale-By-The-Sea is incorporated — has its own government...and you can see these folks are PROUD of their town! Visitors are WELCOME *(many come back here to live)*, but you wont' see the *hordes* that you do elsewhere. You can WALK to *any place in town,* and it's an EASY DRIVE to *all the nearby attractions!!!*

A1A Lauderdale-By-The-Sea, FL   Open Daily   FREE

VENICE U.S.A.

With 300 M-I-L-E-S of boating canals and waterways it is no wonder that the *"transport of choice"* in Ft. Lauderdale is the jaunty bobbing WATER TAXI'S!! They splash through 165 miles of waterways....Over 44,000 resident mega-yacht & cruiser owners sail these waters. Ft. Lauderdale is a *global tourist destination* with several elaborate revitalizations already "complete"!! Most popular near (5 mile oceanfront) is the "Sculptured" WAVE-LINE PROMENADE. The 12 foot width invites walkers bikers & skaters. I most enjoyed RIVERWALK...It's a *sensational green linear park* on New River (both sides)! Many waterside dining cafes and similar to New York City during "peak hours" you may have to wait for a taxi...water taxi... of course!! Several strolling sites along Riverwalk are: Cooley's Landing, Downtown Dock Facility, Birch las Olas Moorings and stunning MUSEUM OF ART! Many *old neighborhoods* have 1930's architectural "MIX". One such is historic residential area of SAILBOAT BEND. Home districts upgraded by blocking off streets, extensive tree-rescue and beautifying existing structures — If you're a "boat-nut" and like excitement visit Ft. Lauderdale in the fall when it hosts the annual 5-day WORLD's LARGEST IN-WATER INTERNATIONAL BOAT SHOW — you'll go "bonkers". Downtown Area is a happy "Pandora's Box" of the unexpected — I saw several wild parrots peering out of trees, a still operative SWING BRIDGE over New River and if you "cotton" to old world elegance you'll enjoy staying at HISTORIC RIVERSIDE HOTEL!!!

RIVERSIDE HOTEL (954) 467-0671   FT. LAUDERDALE, FL   800-325-3280
WATER TAXI (954) 467-6677   DOWNTOWN - NEW RIVER   OPEN DAILY

Classic Churches

ST. GABRIEL'S EPISCOPAL CHURCH
OH, THOSE MAGNIFICENT WINDOWS!

"Neo" may mean NEW, but ST. GABRIEL'S EPISCOPAL CHURCH is over a CENTURY *old!!* Built in 1887, this *Neo-Gothic* house of worship is the OLDEST church in Titusville, founded by *Mary Titus,* wife of the man who gave the city its name. Its *unique architecture features five gables on each side* and TWENTY *magnificent stained glass windows!* Take *special* notice of the large window at the *back,* depicting a LIGHT-HOUSE at the edge of the mighty Atlantic. It's dedicated to the memory of MILLS BURN-HAM, Keeper of the Cape Canaveral light house *for 36 years.* He died in 1886, just before the church was begun. In addition to those windows, the interior of St. Gabriel's has some *outstanding wood-work* in the altar rail, the kneelers and even the collection boxes. Look for the *chocolate-brown edifice* on Pine Street, across from Brevard County Courthouse.

TITUSVILLE, FL PINE ST.   OPEN - SUNDAY

ST. EDWARD'S CATHOLIC CHURCH
DEDICATED TO ST. EDWARD THE CONFESSOR

St. Edward's is a TREASURE!! Overhead hang FOUR *crystal chandeliers* — honest! The MAIN ALTAR must be *30 feet high* and is of CARRARA MARBLE *beautifully carved.* Flanking this are the VIRGIN and ST. JOSEPH altars.   There are *45 exquisite stained glass windows* and the CEILING!!! *Each square was hand-cast and painted,* then INDIVIDUALLY ATTACHED! MAG-NIFICENT!!! Notice the HUGE PIPE ORGAN — bet that makes gorgeous music! Built in 1927, the architecture of St. Edward's is SPANISH RENAISSANCE with Spanish tile roof. Notice the domed SOUTH TOWER and the lower NORTH TOWER which is crowned by an ARCADE. Special SODIUM VAPOR HIGH WATTAGE LAMPS *have been installed outside at the corners of the church. These can be seen many miles out to sea* and by *pilots approaching the airport at night. Special note:* on the *north side* of the church, *8th pew from the rear,* a PLAQUE reads, "President John F. Kennedy knelt here at Mass."

PALM BEACH, FL 144 N. COUNTY RD.   (561) 832-0400
OPEN DAILY   FREE

BETHESDA-BY-THE-SEA —
MONUMENT TO INTERNATIONAL FRIENDSHIP

Bethesda-By-The-Sea, the name of this INSPIRING Episcopal Church, means "THE HOUSE OF HEALING BY THE SEA." Although the first church was built in 1889, this soaring GOTHIC structure rose in 1925 in the style of LEON CATHEDRAL, *considered the most beautiful church in*

Spain! Bethesda is constructed of CAST STONES which were *molded on the premises!!* The interior is EXQUISITE with truly MAGNIFICENT STAINED GLASS WINDOWS. *Take special notice* of the TE DEUM WINDOW above the High Altar in the Chancel. Such JEWEL TONES!!! The REREDOS (altar screens) behind the High Altar are *carved* in WHITE LIMESTONE. To the left you'll see the PARALYTIC at the POOL OF BETHESDA where Jesus heals him. This is the MIRACLE for which the church is named. As you pass through the beautiful GARTH (courtyard), you'll see in the North Cloister Wall the POOL OF BETHESDA with a lovely PINK LIMESTONE ANGEL. From the garth, walk thought the *East Arcade* to the CLUETT MEMORIAL GARDENS. They are BREATH-TAKING!!! The gardens are open 8 a.m. to 5 p.m.

(561) 655-4554
Palm Beach FL 5 County Rd   Open Daily   Free

ST. BERNARD de CLAIRVAUX — SPANISH MONASTERY

Monastery and cloisters were built in 1133 in Segovia, Spain. *Cistercian monks* lived and worked within these walls for 700 years. In 1925 W.R. Hearst bought the monastery and cloisters for $500,000. Structures were dismantled, numbered and packed in 11,000 crates for shipment to the U.S. In New York, workmen unpacked the stones with no thought to which crate the stones came out of...thus was created the world's LARGEST JIGSAW PUZZLE, which took 19 months and $1,500,000 to put back together! The CLOISTERS are early Gothic. Some of the MANY ARTIFACTS are Pope's Cabinet (1623-1644) for vestments, original wrought-iron gate (250 pounds), Ten Corbels (shields) of the Noble Families. the FRENCH ALTAR was carved in Cannes. Notice *vaulted ceilings* in the CHAPTER HOUSE where the monks held choir practice. You'll see Flemish paintings of 1470, and 800-year-old BAPTISMAL FONT (still used) and a white Italian marble relief carved in the 1600's. Be sure to stroll THE GARDEN WALK of over 1000 plants and trees!!

North Miami Beach FL Dixie Hwy. at 167th St.   Admission
Open Daily 10-4 Sun. noon-4   (305) 945-1462

Everglades Mystique

OUR FLORIDA TREASURE

Whichever the season for an Everglades visit, one must come away with a sense of *wonder*. 1,000,000 people visit the park each year. It is suggested, if possible, to see the park during winter, *December through March.* If your tour can only be made in summer months — April through November, be sure to take insect repellent for mosquito protection. They can be fierce. Also wear loose-fitting shirt and long, baggy pants and wide-brimmed hat for the sun. Don't forget camera and binoculars.

A SPECIAL RIVER

It is 6 inches deep and over 50 miles wide. Everglades means "marshy land of tall grass". Best way to see portion of these 2,000,000 acres is to WALK. ROYAL PALM AND FLAMINGO are *2 best visitor's centers* for entering this wet and dry habitat. I recommend any or ALL of 6 TRAILS: The Anhinga, Gumbo Limbo, Pineland, Pa-hay-okee Overlook, Mahogany Hammock and West Lake Tails. Do see DWARF CYPRESS FOREST. These small cypress are over 100 years old, found near the 3-foot limestone ridge of Rock Reef Pass. COOT BAY POND and MRAZEK POND offer fine bird watching. *A wilderness waterway* squirms (99 miles) about estuarian areas. There are 5 shorter canoe trails for the less hearty. I enjoyed "Flamingo" because of the 'EXTRAS". Count'em (Tram tours, boat tours, motel, campground, boat rentals, marina and restaurant). Get MAPS at visitor centers. Bird sightings best in WINTER!!

HOMESTEAD, FL   (941) 695-3101
OPEN DAILY SUNUP-SUNSET   ADMISSION

SHARK VALLEY BIKE LOOP — HIKING PATH — TRAM TOUR

Pick one of three activities above, proceed at leisure. A delightful *15-mile loop road* guides visitors through hardwood hammocks, freshwater sloughs and grassy plains. An *observation tower* at road's end gives inspiring views. Possibility of high water during certain seasons makes advance info advisable. Everglades Loop permits one to get an authentic *feel* of the Everglades. bring lunch. BIKE RENTALS ARE AVAILABLE. Remember sun hat, binoculars and camera. In 1994 I counted 53 GATORS at Shark Valley!

30 mi. east of Everglades City, FL   Open 8-6 Daily
ADMISSION   (305) 221-8776

OASIS STATION TRAIL

When completed the Florida trail will extend 1300 miles throughout the state. An exciting portion is located in *Everglades Big Cypress Preserve*. Almost 30 miles can be hiked from the *Oasis Ranger Station* on U.S. 41 all the way to Alligator Alley. Most people prefer a shorter 1 to 5 mile walk. Try to do any hiking in winter — December through March. Otherwise, mosquitoes may make you *detrail*. The walk will traverse cypress stands, freshwater marl prairies,and hardwood hammocks. Birds, animals and wildflowers are here to be admired. Stop at the *ranger station* for maps and info.

13 miles east of Ochopee, FL on U.S. 41 (239) 695-4111
OPEN YEAR' ROUND   FREE

10,000 ISLANDS

Everglades City is a stepping-off point into another world. The national park maintains a *Visitor Center* and conducts *boat tours* through this fascinating island water world. Sometimes *porpoise* frolic beside the craft. Birdlife, seen at close range, includes osprey, American bald eagle, great snowy white herons, *pink spoonbills* and so many more. Summertime brings *gators* out to bask in the sun. The wilderness tour glides through mangrove tunnels, *Indian shell mounds* and mazes of curving mangrove jungle creeks and rivers. There is a 2 1/2-hour trip which stops for shelling on a small gulf island or a 1 3/4-hour trip with no stop.

Everglades City, FL 30 mi. So. of Naples   (941) 695-2591
OPEN DAILY   ADMISSION BOAT TOUR

FAKAHATCHEE STRAND

"A strand is an elongated 'SWAMP FOREST" which is readily visible on the horizon in contrast to the surrounding grassy savannas. *Fakahatchee Strand* is 20 miles long and 3 to 5 miles wide. Its forest is most unusual because of the mixed growth of royal palms, bald cypress and epiphytics (orchids, mosses and lichens). Fakahatchee is home to Florida black bear, fox, mink and the almost extinct Florida panther (Between 20-30 left). Many strands are clearly visible from U.S. 41. The *boardwalk* is entered through a canopy of green low-hanging trees next to an Indian village. You may drive or stroll to the boardwalk. This is a 2000-foot meandering walk through a swamp jungle which is one of the *rarest* in the world. It is virtually the same since the first Europeans arrived in America. You will see giant fern sometimes reaching 10 feet, royal palms, strangler figs, orchids, air plants and a diversity of rare vegetation. An interpretive booklet is available at the boardwalk.

BIG CYPRESS BEND U.S. 41   OPEN DAILY
SEVEN MILES WEST OF SR 29   FREE

EVERGLADES CITY — PAST ECHOES

Collier's *"Company Town", gateway to* the Everglades, and fishing village par excellence. It is all these and more. Crab pots floating in roadside canals are indicative of the community's livelihood. Unexpected *wide boulevards* having grassy palm-lined medians first greet the visitor on Collier Ave. This is because Everglades was a *planned town* built on filled land in the 1920's. It was to be Collier's *control center* for building the Tamiami Trail linking Tampa and Miami. A *charming 3-story white hotel* once stood on Broadway Ave. The lower floor contained a general store selling everything from guns to Indian craft articles. The bustling little town of yesterday even had its own trolley line. Alas, no more! Remnants of that progressive time are still evident in old metal lamp posts topped by large white globes. *These line most city streets.* Drive to the west end of Broadway and follow *Riverside Drive.* It winds along the water leading to the Intracoastal Waterway, and is bordered by stilt homes (sky houses), banyan trees and other pretties. Everglades preserves its heritage in two more historic buildings. Both at juncture of Broadway and Storter Aves. — one being the *old Bank of Everglades,* another is the 1928 *Company Laundry building.* Don't rush your visit. Overnight if you like. There are fine resorts and restaurants. Best comes last. FISHING, FISHING, FISHING.

EVERGLADES CITY FL SO. OF US 41 ON SR 29
OPEN DAILY   FREE

Fishing

CAUSEWAY ANGLING

No fooling around! Fishings is SERIOUS BUSINESS here and the locals sport "heavy equipment" to prove it!! TWO BRIDGES span the Indian River where *cast netting and pole fishing* holds way. Bustling boat ramps lie beside sheltered *lunch tables* smack-dab on the seawall where vigilant PELICANS eye your every movement...watch 'em — they're dinner-stealers... FESTIVALS are held on this causeway, thus the GRANDSTANDS! On the west side scores of craft bob at anchor making the scene especially restful.

JENSEN BEACH FL CAUSEWAY RD. 732
OPEN DAILY   ADMISSION FREE

LITTLE JIM BRIDGE — WHERE FISH MEETS HOOK

As you travel the Treasure Coast down A1A, about 2 miles north of Ft. Pierce center you'll come to NORTH BEACH CAUSEWAY. A left turn here will take you to LITTLE JIM BRIDGE where the serious FISHERFOLK congregate. There are actually TWO bridges: a 90-year-old WOODEN bridge and a newer CEMENT one. *Both are in use.* Bring a folding chair if you're bound for the *old bridge*, where you can sit and dangle a line for a variety of the finny fellas. On the littler cement bridge, you'll be about 15-20 feet off the water, so you won't need a *snatch hook*. On the west side of Little Jim's Bridge is LITTLE JIM'S JOINT where you can pick up *sandwiches and your favorite quaffs* when the "hungries" growl!! There's a *public park* for PICNICKING and *phones* handy if you want to call home to say *"they're biting"*, so you'll be late!

DIRECTIONS ABOVE   OPEN DAWN TO DUSK
FT. PIERCE FL   FREE

OLD WABASSO BRIDGE — A GOOD PLACE TO DROP THE HOOK

Hook, line and sinker, that is! TROUT and LADYFISH are to be had here on an *incoming tide*. There's parking on the east and west sides of the bridge, so if FISHING'S your thing, try OLD WABASSO BRIDGE!! *Live shrimp* is the *bait of choice* — you can buy 'em at any of the numerous bait shops in the area, or if you feel *adventuresome,* you can try NETTING YOUR OWN from the river. Good luck!!

WABASSO FL RD 510   OPEN DAILY
                                                     FREE

SOUTH JETTY PARK — A GEM ON THE TREASURE COAST

This is one NEAT PLACE!! The JETTIES reach *waaay out into the ocean* and the day I stopped, there were FISHERFOLK on every side!!! A boardwalk parallels the sand and you can watch the SURF *crashing against the rocks by the inlet*.. There are sheltered PICNIC TABLES right smack on top of the jetties and you can grill hot dogs, hamburgers, steaks — *whatever suits your fancy!* Or you can eat at the RAW BARS, SEAFOOD RESTAURANTS or SANDWICH SHOPS which abound here. One local eatery has a PARROT — a real talker — outside to greet all comers! There are green PICNIC PARKS here, nice modest motels, even apartments for a longer stay. The INDIAN RIVER MARINE SCIENCE CENTER is located here as well. Just north of the causeway at the Peter B. Cobb Bridge is CAUSEWAY ISLAND. *It's covered with green trees,* but in the evening when hundreds of PELICANS come home to roost, it looks like a SNOW MOUNTAIN!!! South Jetty Park has free parking for about 100 cars.

S-A1A (OCEAN DRIVE) FT. PIERCE, FL   OPEN DAILY   FREE

DEERFIELD INTERNATIONAL FISH PIER
FISH AROUND THE CLOCK —

It's 720 feet long and 20 years young, this Deerfield International Fishing Pier!! And boy, do the *fisherfolk* congregate here!!! It's open 24 HOURS year 'round and you can go for everything that BITES....EXCEPT SHARK. That's a NO-NO! If you don't want to fish, you can watch the RACING BOATS *hurtling over the water!* And if Mr. CHARLES THOMP- SON, father of the fish pier, happens to be around, you might want to have a chat with him. He's quite a COLORFUL CHARACTER!! There's a loudspeaker system *in case you get a call from home* and special parking for pier patrons. Real handy is a little SQUARE where you can pick up all sorts of SNACK MEALS: pizzas, subs, hot dogs — you name it, it's HERE!!!

R-810 OFF A1A   DEERFIELD BEACH, FL   OPEN DAILY   ADMISSION

POMPANO MUNICIPAL FISH PIER — IT IS LONG

Twenty-seven years ago, this humongous POMPANO FISH PIER rose over the green Atlantic — 1080 FEET OF IT!!! It's the LONGEST and STRONGEST fish pier in South Florida! It's a 3-SHIFT pier, open 24 hours — *even the* PELICANS *take their shift!!!* They have a TACKLE & BAIT SHOP here — you need it, they've got it! POMPANO and MACKEREL head the list — BUT just before I was here, a TEENAGER drug in a 30-POUND SNOOK!!! If you get tired of fishing, there are COFFEE BENCHES, and if the "hungries" hook you, take your pick of 4 OUTDOOR CAFES or FISHERMAN'S WHARF SEAFOOD RESTAURANT & LOUNGE. There's even a RAW BAR!! A book- stall offers books on the bunch of different subjects — SHELLS, FISHING, BIRDS — you name it!! *Last but not least*, every, Monday and Tuesday, there's a LIMBO CONTEST!!! You READY?!!

222 POMPANO BEACH BL.   POMPANO BEACH, FL   OPEN DAILY   FREE

BLUE CYPRESS LAKE & STICK MARSH

The lake is 6,554 acres and has the *"hollywood"* fish (largemouth bass) in quantity. Trophy months are Dec.-April — a recent 6 week period posted 66 bass weighing 10 lbs. or more. I'm not a fisherman — would I lie??? Lake is scenic ringed by cypress with a wee park near boatramp. *Fish attractors* help catches of specks, bluegill and shellcrackers. You may hook the "funny- looking" GARFISH, my favorite table fish. If deep-fried it tastes like a cross of shrimp & chicken. Use shrimp sauce dips and you've a yummy meal!! STICK MARSH is *new*. Only flooded in 1987 in order to return St. Johns River to its original state it is now a "hot spot" of the bass circuits. By 1988 the marsh deepened to 6 ft. There are lots of canals and marsh is dotted with tall dead tree trunks State biologists found that marsh bass have a growth rate *(3 times) that of other lake bass*. Four years after stocking aver- age bass are 4 & 5 pounds! Take time to see neat (town?) of FELLSMERE 1910. It was settled by Fell an English mining engineer who served the Czar of Russia! Middleton Fish Camp, (561) 778-0150, Rentals & Guide

VERO BEACH, FL BLUE CYPRESS RD 60 OPEN DAILY
FELLSMERE, FL STICK MARSH RD 512 RD TO C-54 CANAL 11 MILES

Flea Markets

FESTIVAL FLEA MARKET

World's apart from any flea mart I've attended . . . . and I'm the champ. What's the diff??? O.K. one outstanding feature. It is indoors and AIR CONDITIONED. It is blocks long. Nearly 675 merchants sell names you'll recognize at below outlet prices. I live 140 miles from FESTIVAL but get there at least 2 times yearly. I take my sister and after 2-1/2 hours I (d-r-a-g) her out or "other way 'round". I enjoy dickering with vendors . . . . Buying in multiples gets their attention. Purchased lucite items items at 25% less. If you know retail prices you clean up! Infinite lunch choices at international food courts. Market has full service beauty salon, video arcade (park kids), and 8 screen movie theater. Even the CADILLAC crowd shops here!!! Place on overdrive at Christmas season----wear your elbow & knee bumpers.

POMPANO, FL SAMPLE RD (2 MILES WEST OF I-95) EXIT 69
OPEN-TUES - FRI (9:30-5) SAT & SUN (9:30-6)
OPEN-CHRISTMAS & NEW YEARS DAY   (954) 979-4555

THUNDERBIRD SWAP SHOP — A REAL EXTRAVAGANZA

70 ACRES of it — the *largest flea market in the southeastern U.S.!!* It's an *indoor/outdoor affair* — outside, canopies shelter browsers and buyers. You'll see typical *garage sale stuff,* some *antiques* plus a broad range of *new items.* Inside, *90-100 vendors* offer everything from *brand-name shoes, clothes, jewelry, pottery* — you name it!! Food concessions offer INTERNATIONAL goodies: *French, German, Greek, Oriental...* or, if that's not your thing, there's a snack bar *American style!!* Plenty of REST AREAS here if you want to *make a day of it.* There is a $1 WEEKEND ONLY *parking charge,* otherwise it's FREE!! The INDOOR SWAP SHOP is open Wed.-Fri. 8 a.m.-4 p.m., weekends 8 a.m.-6 p.m. The OUTDOOR MARKET is open Wed.-Sun. 6 a.m.-4 p.m.

3121 W. SUNRISE BLVD., FT. LAUDERDALE, FL (954) 791-7927   FREE

SUPER FLEA AND FARMERS MARKET

I can't help myself. I'm "nuts" about flea markets!! And if one just pops up on a highway I'm driving, teams of oxen couldn't pull me past it. SUPER F. is on 20 acres. Been here since 1987. Has 900 booths, 2 snack shacks, all under cover with raised cement platform walkways... Newly added added is an ANTIQUE SECTION! Fire up that "chariot", get addicted like me.

MELBOURNE, FL I-95 EXIT 72 (WEST SIDE)   (321) 242-9124
OPEN FRI-SAT-SUN 9-4   FREE

Botanical Gardens

THE BOTANICAL GARDENS
AT FLORIDA INSTITUTE OF TECHNOLOGY

Botanical gardens on a COLLEGE CAMPUS? Yup! *Thirty-five gorgeous acres* of *natural streams,* lush *tropical vegetation* and 2,000 PALM TREES OVER 100 different species!!! Nature trails wander throughout and as you walk along, the words that come to mind are, *"beauty"* and *"serenity"*. There are *surprises* around every bend — even in front of the F.I.T. Administration Building you'll see a *garden of rare herbs and plants.* Located just 3 miles from the heart of Melbourne, the Botanical Gardens are easy to find and *well worth a visit...believe me!!*

800-944-4348

150 W. UNIVERSITY BLVD. MELBOURNE, FL   F.I.T.   (321) 674-8200
OPEN DAWN-DUSK   FREE

THE MORIKAMI MUSEUM, GARDENS AND PARK

PICTURESQUE is hardly the word! This place is SERENELY BEAUTIFUL!!! Nestled on an ISLAND, surrounded by a MOAT is Morikami Museum. Access is via a *pretty Japanese style* FOOTBRIDGE and as you enter the museum's portals, you will be politely asked to *remove you shoes in true* JAPANESE TRADITION! Exhibits highlight Japanese FOLK ARTS, CUSTOMS and outstanding ARTISTS. *Check dates of such special programs* as the TEA CEREMONY and the KIMONO DEMONSTRATION and FASHION SHOW. The GARDENS are very different and so lovely, with ROCKS and TROPICAL PLANTS. A little WATERFALL Cascades down into the moat, which is bordered with POND LILIES. Here swim the *beautiful ornamental* CARP or KOI — like living JEWELS!! A 1 1/2-mile NATURE TRAIL leads through BAMBOOS, AUSSY EUCALYPTUS, PINES and CYPRESS with *many rest stops and picnic areas.* Do bring a picnic lunch for TARRYING. This place deserves to be enjoyed at a LEISURELY pace! Nearby is the BONSAI COLLECTION — and a miniature BANYAN TREE *just begging to have its picture taken!!*

4000 MORIKAMI RD. DELRAY BEACH, FL   (561) 495-0233
OPEN- PARK - DAILY - MUSEUM - TUES.-SAT. 10-5   FREE

PLANTATION HERITAGE PARK — BEAUTY AND ACTION

This is a whatcha call a DOUBLE-BARRELED PARK!! On the one hand, it's a *fantastic* NATURE PRESERVE with an *agricultural-horticultural theme.* You'll see numerous plantings of TROPICAL FLOWERING TREES and PALMS throughout the park. There's also a TRAIL through a grove of mature *tropical fruit trees* and yet another which explores a tropical HARDWOOD HAMMOCK, PINE FLATWOODS and a COASTAL STRAND FOREST! Pick up some ideas for your *home landscaping* from the display of *ferns, bromeliads, herbs and wildflowers.* On the other hand, there's plenty of ACTION to be had! Bike and boat rentals, a 10 station FITNESS COURSE, volleyball, horseshoes and FIVE picnic areas with tables and grills! Lots to SEE and DO at Planation Heritage!! FREE admission weekdays.

1100 S. Fig Tree Lane Planation FL   (954) 791-1025
Open Daily   Weekend Charge

FLAMINGO GARDENS — A TROPICAL PARADISE

Sapodilla, Soursop, Sapote!! What ARE they? TREES...*exotic trees!* You'll see GUMBO LIMBOS, now a rarity in so much of Florida, and a 200-YEAR-OLD STAND OF OAK!!! There are 22 CHAMPION TREES, so honored because they're the LARGEST OF THEIR KIND IN FLORIDA!!! Example: a CLUSTER FIG 105 FEET TALL and 45 FEET AROUND!! That's BIG! *Bring your cameras!* Flamingo Gardens truly is a *paradise*...perfect for a FAMILY OUTING! Take a TRAM RIDE through citrus groves and the Everglades jungle! Kids will love the PETTING ZOO with PYGMY GOATS and BARBADOS SHEEP and GATOR WORLD with RARE CROCODILES, MONKEYS and gorgeous TROPICAL BIRDS!! Wander along the paths of the BOTANICAL GARDENS...*so beautiful!* Visit the Everglades Museum with *Seminole artifacts,* and the Transportation Museum which features *antique cars, airboats and swamp buggies!*

3750 Flamingo Rd., Ft. Lauderdale, FL   (954) 473-0010
Open Daily 9-5   Admission

SPRING FEVER—ALL YEAR

Oriental *Japanese Gardens* are the heart of these botanicals. Attention to details of line patterns, water movement and plant positioning are keys to Japanese garden design... The BONSAI DISPLAY is especially pleasurable. Gardens date from 1948 but open to the public since 1985. You'll enjoy the *Herb Gardens* as well as the Palm Section Walk. Newly opened is the ecological Native Plant Landscaping Area. For a small (a bit under 4 acres) garden, HEATHCOTE BOTANICAL GARDENS, is making a name for itself. production greenhouse grows flowers and foliage of "subtropics" (Orchids, too)... On grounds are a library giftshop and historic 1922 Carlton House. Buy plants??? Sure Can!!!

Ft. Pierce Fl 210 Savannah Rd   (772) 464-4672
Open Tues.-Sat. 9-5 Sun (Nov-Apr) 1-5   Admission

Hikin' Bikin' Paddlin' Saddlin'

TREE TOPS PARK — HORSING AROUND

"Take nothing but memories, leave nothing but footprints" is the MOTTO of Broward parks. You'll take plenty of HAPPY MEMORIES away from Tree Tops! Located on part of the *historical ridge system* called the

PINE ISLANDS, Tree Tops is *257 acres of natural beauty* ...with winding NATURE TRAILS, a 28-FOOT OBSERVATION TOWER at the highest point in the park — *bring your camera!!!* BRIDLE PATHS wander for more than 3 SCENIC MILES...or you can rent a canoe or pedal boat and cruise the CANALS or LAKES!! FISHING, PICNICKING, a PLAYGROUND for the kiddos...it's all there to enjoy! Planning a WEDDING? *Talk to the man in charge* about TREE TOPS CENTER! Nestled in an OAK HAMMOCK all secluded, it's a NATURAL!!!

3900 S.W. 100TH AVE. DAVIE, FL   (954) 370-3750
OPEN DAILY 8-5   WEEKEND CHARGE

TRADEWINDS PARK BIKING — ROWING — PETTING

Talk about RUSTIC CHARM! Tradewinds has it — 540 *beautiful acres of trees, lakes and ponds*...and LOADED with activities!!! This park is in *two sections* on either side of Sample Road...and there's *plenty of parking in 8 paved lots!!* You wanna FISH? Go to it! Or how about BOATING? Rent a canoe or a pedal boat and take your pick of *three different locations!* There's BIKE rentals, too, and an 18-hole mini-golf course!! THREE RAISED BOARDWALK NATURE TRAILS meander through the park. the longest, 3000 FEET, winds through a *cypress and maple stand — the largest in the county!!* And for you FITNESS FANS there's a JOGGING and POWER FITNESS course running along next to the bike path!! Take a look at the old preserved WINDMILL which still pumps water...and meet KIMBERLY, the 700-lb. PIG in the Petting Zoo!!! On weekends you can enjoy PONY RIDES and guided HORSEBACK RING!! 'Bout the only thing you can't do here is swim! Picnic tables, grills, food concessions, a general store...*everything you need to make a day of it!*

3600 W. SAMPLE RD. COCONUT CREEK, FL   WEEKEND CHARGE
OPEN DAILY 8-5   (954) 968-3880

C.B. SMITH PARK — LOTS OF LAKES

Don't know who Mister Smith is, but he sure has some PARK! Sixty acres of LAKES and THREE MILES of CANOE TRAILS!! *Rent a boat and paddle to your heart's content!* Shoreside your thing? Rent a bike—or ROLLER SKATES and head down the 2 1/2-mile *bike and skate trail!!!* DON'T MISS the 50-FT. HIGH WATER SLIDE with *700 thrilling feet of* TURNS, DROPS and TUNNELS...or the 400-FT. TUBE RIDE!!! There's a MODEL-BOAT BASIN, too, plus *playgrounds, horseshoe pitches, volleyball courts, a basketball court* and HUNDREDS of picnic tables and grills!! Even FREE TRAM SERVICE weekends and holidays!!! SEE MAP PG. 58

900 N. FLAMINGO RD. PEMBROKE, FL   (954) 437-2650
OPEN DAILY 8-8   ADMISSION WEEKENDS

QUIET WATERS PARK — NOT FOR COUCH POTATOES

Quiet Waters is *427 acres of fun for the whole family!!* SWIMMING? You bet! BIKE rentals, BOAT rentals... super CATFISH, BREAM and BASS fishing! *Catch your lunch and cook it on the GRILL in the picnic area!* Mini-golf, playground, 2 food concessions and SKI-RIXEN CABLE WATER SKIING!!! It's safe, it's fun — *a thrill a minute!!!* Last but not least, Quiet Waters has TENTING CAMPGROUNDS!! You can bring your own or take advantage of the unique RENT-A-CAMP package. Call for detailed info.

6601 N. POWERLINE RD., DEERFIELD BEACH, FL   (954) 360-1315
OPEN DAILY 8-5   ADMISSION WEEKENDS

WEST LAKE PADDLING — PLENTY OF ACTION

This is a UNIQUE park! Part of its *1,300 acres* is a MANGROVE PRE-SERVE teeming with ANIMAL, BIRD and PLANT LIFE including some rare ENDANGERED species!! Another section of West Lake is PEOPLE-ORIENTED! RACQUETBALL and TENNIS COURTS — FOUR OF EACH!!! A *jogging trail* and VITA-COURSE with *10 stations* to tone up all those MUSCLES!! Take a spin on the BIKE path or try your skill at HORSESHOES or VOLLEYBALL! Picnic tables and grills are scattered throughout the park and *if you want to get out on the water,* rent a boat and paddle around the 10-ACRE LAKE!!

1200 SHERIDAN ST. HOLLYWOOD, FL   (954) 926-2410
OPEN DAILY 8-8   ADMISSION WEEKENDS

TOPEEKEEGEE YUGNEE PARK —A TONGUE TWISTER

Topeekeegee Yugnee is SEMINOLE for a *gathering place! But don't even TRY to pronounce it! Just do as the locals do and call it T.Y. Park!! And DON'T MISS IT!! Take a dip in the clear blue* FALLING WATERS SWIMMING LAGOON with its *white sandy beaches!* There's even a special CHILDREN'S AREA with FOUNTAINS and SLIDES!! Whiz down the TWISTING WATERS FLUME RIDE— *50 feet high, 700 feet of drops, tunnels and turns!* Shoreside activities feature a *3-mile jog, bike and roller-skating trail* plus an *18-hole mini-golf course... basketball and volleyball courts* — even a VIDEO GAME ROOM!!! *Plenty* of picnic tables and grills AND a food concession and trading post where you can *pick up the Necessaries!*

SHERIDAN ST. & N. PARK RD. HOLLYWOOD, FL   (954) 985-1980
OPEN DAILY 8-8   ADMISSION

MARKHAM PARK — HIT THE BULLSEYE!

Tired of the beach? *Head for Markham!!!* This is a 665-acre park with a DIFFERENCE! Sure, there's fishing, canoe rentals *(plus a boat ramp so you can launch your own craft),* BUT how about a MODEL AIRPLANE FIELD!! OR an 86-acre MILLION DOLLAR TARGET RANGE!! It's a *complete gun range* with PRO SHOP and concessions! Try your hand at RIFLE, PISTOL, SKEET or TRAP SHOOTING! Or, maybe you prefer ARCHERY! (Call 305/384-7010 for info.) For quieter pursuits, walk along the beautiful NATURE TRAIL ATOP THE LEVEE...*it's right next to the* EVERGLADES!! You'll see *ferns, willowheads and a bunch of other plants, birds and critters.* For CAMPERS, 86 RENTAL SITES which can be *reserved by phone.*

16001 W. S.R. 84 SUNRISE, FL   (954) 389-2000
OPEN DAILY 8-5   ADMISSION WEEKENDS

A+ BICYCLING 57,892 ACRES

Choices for ALL...lollygagers, (me), distance riders or mountain bikers. Entering at NORTH GRADE puts riders next to a lengthy scenic canal bordered by *extensive greens for picnics* or "angling". A bit of canopy appears "here-n-there, also stately Cypress Domes. Lots of botanicals to admire... ferns, willow & bay and unusual Java Plum trees planted in the 50's! EXCELLENT WILDLIFE OBSERVATION. Deer are not sissypants. they were as curious to ogle me as I was to gawk at them. Much exotic "Life On The Wing" too!! Abundant wildflowers (pink, yellows, whites) on *Tomato Field Grade*. This was a surprise during late June rain season — Yellow flies were a bit pesky! At the end of SOUTH GRADE is a water control structure and a W-I-D-E (6 mile canal) full of bass & 'gators. Dike is elevated here with one high overlook affording a *vista* of about 15 miles away... STUMPER'S GRADE is an interesting cycling experience — within 6 miles I counted 45 curves!! Part of J.W. CORBETT WILDLIFE MANAGEMENT AREA is Everglades Conservation Youth Camp where I saw about 90 "Munchkins" learning to swim, canoe and become future solid citizens...Councilors looked "stressed-out"!! SEE MAP PAGE. 64

PALM BEACH GARDENS FL   FL GAME & FRESH WATER FISH COMMISSION
JUNCTURE OF RDS 710 & 706 OR NORTHLAKE BL
OPEN — DAILY-NOT HUNT DAYS   FREE   (561) 625-5122

Historic Homes and Hotels

GRANT HOUSE — DOWN BY THE RIVERSIDE

Go see how Florida folks *used to live* 'way back when. GRANT HOUSE says it all. A restored HISTORICAL LANDMARK, this *1916 charmer* is located at Fisherman's Landing in — where else but Grant. It has to be one of the *most peaceful settings on earth*. Green lawn, lovely plantings, a boardwalk to a *wee lagoon* spanned by a footbridge which leads to a *nature walk among live oaks*. The small white house with shutters at the windows is raised up on *blocks* in case of floods — the way they built 'em in those days. The *homey front porch* with its rockers overlooks a beautiful little beach and a *100-foot dock*. Like the front, the back porch also has a river view. Inside, notice the *beautiful lace curtains* as you wander through... and the *cozy kitchen* with its wooden icebox and cooper kettles. In the bedrooms, you'll see the *old iron bedsteads* with their quilts. Notice the high ceilings AND the sign at the front door which requests, *"Clean shirt and shoes, please"!!!* It's a gentle get-away, folks. Enjoy!

FISHERMAN'S LANDING GRANT, FL
OPEN 10-4, MON.-SAT.   ADMISSION DONATION

GARDNER HOUSE — THE WAY FOLKS USED TO LIVE

Here, by gum is an honest-to--gosh CRACKER HOUSE! You've heard of 'em, now you'll SEE one! Located under the *Peter B. Cobb Bridge on South Causeway,* on the grounds of the St. Lucie Historical Museum, this 1907 *charmer* was built by one *Almand Register,* a barrel-maker or cooper. It's a small white house with wooden shakes, *a friendly porch* with rocking chairs and all surrounded by a *white picket fence!!* There's a reconstructed WATER TOWER on the property as well as a WINDMILL turning just as it did at the turn of the century. Gardner House gets its name from the *Maurice Gardner family* who donated it to *St. Lucie County.* Restoration was completed in 1987 and today you'll see *"living history"* demonstrations depicting the LIFESTYLE of those by-gone days! You might want to *brown-bag* it out on the grounds and enjoy the lovely WATER VIEWS with *boats of every size and description!* It's all a neat look at the early 20th century and remember: *this is not a replica but the real thing!!!*

DIRECTIONS ABOVE FT. PIERCE, FL   (561) 468-1795
OPEN TUES.-SAT. 10-4 SUN. 12-4   ADMISSION

DUBOIS HOME — A FAMILY HISTORY

It sits HIGH ON AN ANCIENT INDIAN MOUND, this *1890's dwelling of the Dubois Family.* Composed of *centuries-old debris* of the JAEGA INDIANS, the mound was purchased by HARRY DUBOIS in 1896 for a homesite. two years later, he built a CYPRESS WOOD house for his wife, SUSAN and their four children — JOHN, HENRY, ANNA and NEIL. *Today, the snug homestead looks much as it did when the family lived there,* with many of the ORIGINAL FURNISHINGS in place. Harry's HIGH SCHOOL CERTIFICATE hangs on one wall, while on the floor are CROCHETED RUGS made by *Susan and Anna. Take special notice of the* BED COVER containing over 1300 PIECES, ALL HANDMADE!!! There's a lot of FAMILY HISTORY here!

DUBOIS RD. JUPITER FL   (561) 747-6639
OPEN SUN. 1-4   ADMISSION

THE BREAKERS HOTEL — STEEPED IN TRADITION

Sheer, gorgeous LUXURY! That's the ONLY way to describe *The Breakers of Palm Beach!* From the *lush, manicured grounds* to the stunning *interior, no detail has been overlooked!!!* Like the PHOENIX of Legend, The Breakers *rose from the ashes of a disastrous* FIRE in 1925 which leveled the old wood structure. It was redesigned and built of fireproof materials in just over ELEVEN MONTHS at the cost of — are you ready? —$6 MILLION! *The exterior* of the new Breakers was inspired (and that's the word) by the famed VILLA MEDICI in Florence. The interior is graced by CRYSTAL CHANDELIERS from VENICE and VIENNA, pink TENNESSEE MARBLE and the CEILINGS are *literally works of art:* 75 ARTISANS *from Europe* created those *magnificent paintings!!! A fountain plays and flowers bloom* in the MEDITERRANEAN COURTYARD *creating romantic ambiance.* During Season, HIGH TEA is served in the NORTH LOGIA *every afternoon at four* — maybe you'd like to PARTAKE!!

SOUTH COUNTY RD. PALM BEACH, FL   (561) 655-6611
OPEN DAILY FREE   (800) 833-3141

WHITEHALL — A NATIONAL TREASURE

Step through the *Portals of the Past* at WHITEHALL, the magnificent Henry Morrison Flagler MANSION & MUSEUM! Co-founder of Standard Oil and Railroad Magnate, Henry Flagler was the man who developed Florida's east coast from *Jacksonville to Key West!* In 1901, he built this American TAJ MAHAL for his wife, Mary Lilli Kenan. TODAY, Whitehall looks much as it did then, fully restored, even to many of the original furnishings. There are priceless collections of porcelain, silver, glass, dolls and lace — even family memorabilia — all listed in the *National Register of Historic Places...*and behind the mansion is another goody: *THE RAMBLER,* Flagler's fabulous private railroad car. LUXURY ON WHEELS!!!

PALM BEACH, FL   (561) 655-2833
OPEN TUES.-SAT., 10 A.M.-5 P.M. SUN. NOON-5 P.M.   ADMISSION

BOCA RATON HOTEL AND CLUB
WHERE THE DREAM BEGAN

Elegant! Opulent! Magnificent! It takes ALL of those superlatives to even BEGIN to describe this FABULOUS RESORT! It took MILLIONS to build, but oh, the RESULTS!! A WEALTH OF LUXURY!!! As you drive up the CAMINO REAL, the *striking pink edifice* with its TWIN TOWERS rises ahead in *majestic grandeur. The gorgeously landscaped grounds* with FOUNTAINS, ROYAL PALMS and LUSH PLANTINGS are like one enormous GARDEN! You have a choice of accommodations here: THE CLOISTER of Legend, *the original building,* built in 1926 by Addison Misner (his DREAM INN) with its striking SPANISH architecture *oozes* OLD WORLD CHARM! When completed it was called *the most beautiful building in America!!* ADDISON COURT is designed for business guests, and there are *luxury accommodations* in the 27 story TOWER overlooking *Lake Boca Raton,* the GOLF VILLAS with their 18-*hole championship golf course,* and the European-style BOCA BEACH CLUB with *views of both the ATLANTIC and the ICW.* There are NINE DINING ROOMS, but surely the CATHEDRAL Dining Room with its *golden ambiance* and VAULTED CEILING has to be one of the most ELEGANT *anywhere!* Visit the CURZON GALLERY, located in The Cloister, with its *marvelous works of art!* This is for sure an INTERNATIONAL SPA — you'll hear just about *every language spoken in the world* right here in this HALLMARK OF LUXURY!!!

CAMINO REAL BOCA RATON, FL   (561) 395-3000
RESERVATIONS REQUIRED   800-327-0101
                       TOURS - TUES-1 P.M, (561) 392-3003

KESTER COTTAGES —A LOOK AT OLD POMPANO

The KESTER COTTAGES were *famous* in this area *back in the Twenties.* Two of them have been restored and now house period furnishings and other memorabilia of a *by-gone era.* The first cottage contains an old ICEBOX, and OIL STOVE and an ANTIQUE WALL PHONE!!

In one bedroom is a HAND-CARVED BED!! The second cottage contains a variety of *memorabilia, books and data* all pertaining to *early pioneers* and *historical events.* There's even an 1950 ORGAN!! Located in Old Pompanos RUSTIC PARK on the *Pompano Canal,* the Kester Cottages are open Sept.-May — Mon., Wed. and Sat. Noon to 4 p.m.

18-20 S.E. 3RD AVE. — POMPANO BEACH, FL   (954) 782-3015
OPEN AS ABOVE   ADMISSION — FREE

16TH CENTURY OPULENCE — VIZCAYA

Felt like royalty. All I needed was a CROWN on my head after touring this *extravagant 24-room villa.* It was built in 1916 by James Deering and represents RENAISSANCE, BAROQUE, ROCOCO AND NEOCLASSIC styles. There are 4 treats (the villa, the gardens, the forest, the museum). Vizcaya is Basque, meaning "elevated place"...this is fitting as it *overlooks Biscayne Bay!!* Rooms are chock-full of rich European furniture, tapestries, marble and paintings. Fountains, pools, and statues harmonize to reveal a "princely life" of 4 centuries past!!!

3251 S. MIAMI AVE. – MIAMI, FL   (305) 250-9133
(SOUTH OF RICKENBACKER CAUSEWAY)   ADMISSION
OPEN-DAILY 9:30-4:30

STRANAHAN HOUSE — HISTORIC AND BEAUTIFUL

This is a GEM of a house right on the NEW RIVER! The *oldest structure in Broward County* and listed in the National Register of Historic Places !! Stranahan House was built in 1901 by FRANK STRANAHAN as a *store and trading post,* and became HOME to Frank and his wife, "MISS IVY" in 1906. Notice the beautiful WALLS of DADE COUNTY PINE...so RARE anymore! The house has been restored to the 1813-15 period with handsome VICTORIAN furniture throughout. Each room is a SURPRISE and a DELIGHT!! In one, the TEENIEST TYPEWRITER I ever saw — about 8 inches long, 8 inches wide and IT WORKS!!! In another room, a GORGEOUS WOODEN ROCKING HORSE!! *Period clothing* hangs in the closets, just as if *the Stranahans still lived here.* Don't miss the VIRGINIA ENGLISH GARDEN with its *coral patio* and *lush tropical flowers and greenery!!* Got a *wedding* in your future? This is the place!!! Tie the knot here.

LAS OLAS BLVD. AT NEW RIVER TUNNEL — FT. LAUDERDALE, FL
OPEN WED.-FRI. - 10-4 - SAT. & SUN. 1-4   (954) 524-4736
    ADMISSION

BONNET PLACE — ARTIST'S HEAVEN

This is a MUST! *It's like something out of a fantasy,* but it's REAL!!! This 35-acre estate and DREAM HOUSE was created by *renowned artists* FREDERIC AND EVELYN BARTLETT, following their marriage in 1931. It's tucked away in its own TROPICAL FOREST near *Hugh Taylor Birch Park* on Fort Lauderdale Beach. *So near and yet so far from the everyday world!!!* You'll see Frederic's STUDIO and the ART GALLERIES with MURALS, TAPESTRIES AND ORIGINAL PAINTINGS! There's a

SHELL MUSEUM too, plus gorgeous ANTIQUES and CAROUSEL ANI-
MALS — that's for STARTERS! Enjoy the NATURE TRAILS, exotic
ORCHIDS and other *tropical plants, birds,* a HORSE-DRAWN SURREY
— even WILD MONKEYS!!! Wear *comfy shoes* 'cuz it takes at least
THREE HOURS to see it all — *and you'll want to!!* Bonnet House is list-
ed in the National Register of Historic Places.

900 N. BIRCH RD. — FT. LAUDERDALE, FL   (954) 563-5393
OPEN TUES.-FRI. TOURS 10 & 1 SUN 1&2 (MAY-NOV)

KING-CROMARTY — OLD AND LOVELY

Two storied with a *shake roof, dormers* and *a friendly front porch!!!* It's
right on the New River, built in 1907 by EDWIN KING, one of the city's
EARLY PIONEERS. Now fully restored, it features *artifacts and memorabilia* of those *olden days.* Notice the beautiful BRASS LANTERN an old
black IRON STOVE which was used to heat the front part of the house. In
the kitchen there's and old HAND PUMP — *no faucet's* in those days!!
Look at the OLD PIE CHEST — all the things you see will give you a
CLEAR PICTURE of how those early settlers lived!

229 S.W. 2ND AVE. — FT. LAUDERDALE, FL   (954) 463-4431
OPEN - GROUPS - CALL   ADMISSION

Museums

BREVARD ART CENTER & MUSEUM

If the VISUAL ARTS are your cuppa, then hustle on over to the BRE-
VARD ART CENTER & MUSEUM (BACAM for short)!! Located in *"Old
Eau Gallie,"* one of Melbourne's *historic districts,* BACAM's exhibits cover
a broad spectrum from ANCIENT SCULPTURE to MODERN ART! There
are *rotating exhibits* from the Museum's permanent collection, *touring
exhibitions from major galleries* and *individual showings* of contemporary
art by *recognized artists.* BACAM also offers lectures and films, concerts
and seminars — PLUS an *unusual exhibit* for the *visually handicapped.*
"Outreach" programs offer art education and hands-on workshops for *all
ages.* It's a *fantastic* place to "soak-up-culture"!!

1463 N. HIGHLAND AVE. — MELBOURNE, FL   (321) 242-0737
OPEN TUES.-FRI. 10-4; SAT. 12:30-2:30; SUN. 12-4   FREE

BREVARD MUSEUM & NATURE TRAILS

Small but intriguing!!! Cocoa's BREVARD MUSEUM OF HISTORY &
NATURAL SCIENCE ia a *neat* place to spend a few hours examining a
variety of exhibits which run the gamut from ancient times to the present.
Young 'uns, age 6 to 14, will have a *"hands-on experience"* in the
Smithsonian accredited DISCOVERY ROOM which is entered through a
representation of an AIS dwelling... people who inhabited Brevard County
as late as the 15th Century but whose past s-t-r-e-t-c-h-e-s back to pre-

historic times!! You'll see their artifacts, marine exhibits and shells and *so much more.* There's even an 1880's GENERAL STORE all stocked with wares of the day. Outside, you can stroll any or all of *three* NATURE TRAILS! Stretching over 22 acres, these trails go through *three distinct ecosystems:* a *pine sandhill community,* a *hardwood hammock* and a *freshwater marsh.* One things sure — you'll *leave* knowing a LOT MORE about the history of Brevard County!!!

2201 MICHIGAN AVE. — COCOA, FL   (321) 632-1830
OPEN TUES.-SAT. 10-4; SUN. 1-4; CLOSED MON.   ADMISSION

LIBERTY BELL MUSEUM — GREAT HERITAGE

Just about EVERYBODY in Brevard County got together to bring this *unique museum* into being! F'instance: in 1976, the *school kids* in South Brevard collected the necessary funds to purchase an *uncracked replica* of the LIBERTY BELL!!! Cast by the Whitechapel Bell Foundry in London, Eng., the bell weighs about a TON and is *permanetly mounted* in the center of the museum. Overhead are *12 flags* of the Revolutionary War period and in the Freedom Shrine are *28 full-scale reproductions* of historic documents from the MAYFLOWER COMPACT and Thomas Jefferson's rough draft of the DECLARATION OF INDEPENDENCE to the Instrument of Surrender in the Pacific which officially ended World War !!! There are numerous exhibits and displays as well, conceived and developed by HONOR AMERICA, Inc. This is an *exceptional opportunity* to take a trip into our nation's *past.*

WELLS PARK — 1601 OAK ST. — MELBOURNE, FL   (321) 727-1776
ACCESSIBLE TO HANDICAPPED   OPEN 10-4 MON.-FRI.; 10-2 SAT.

ST. LUCIE HISTORICAL MUSEUM TREASURE ARTIFACTS

Here is the stuff that makes history COME TO LIFE! The GOLDEN GALLEONS EXHIBIT with *actual artifacts* from the SPANISH SILVER FLEET Lost in the *1715 hurricane!! Arms* from OLD FORT PIERCE and the SEMINOLE WARS! *Tools* used in pioneer industries and even an old 1919 AMERICAN-LAFRANCE FIRE ENGINE! Oh, but there's so much more!!! *You'll step back over* 200 YEARS *in time* as you wander from one fan-tastic exhibit to another. Like the diorama of a SEMINOLE INDIAN ENCAMPMENT with a CHICKEE (house) built of those *indestructible palmetto logs* topped by a *palm-frond roof.* Take a look at the *dugout canoe* scraped and burned by TODAY'S Seminoles just as their *ancestors* did hundreds of years ago!! You'll want to visit Gardner House, located on the grounds here (see section 10). It's easy to spend HOURS in this huge museum... ST. LUCIE HISTORICAL MUSEUM. Go lose yourself in our *fascinating* PAST!!!

414 SEAWAY DRIVE —FT. PIERCE, FL   (772) 462-1795
OPEN TUES.-SAT. 10-4; SUN. 12-4   ADMISSION

ELLIOTT MUSEUM — RECOGNITION OF A GENIUS

Ever see a QUADRICYCLE? You will here!!! Elliott Museum was built by *Harmon P. Elliott* in honor of his father, STERLING ELLIOTT. This *famous American inventor* created the quadricycle in 1886, incorporating in it many features found in the modern AUTOMOBILE!! He also invented the FIRST ADDRESSING MACHINE and the FIRST KNOT-TYING MACHINE! Altogether, father and son held 222 PATENTS and *Elliott Museum has its share on display.* There are *many other exhibits,* all out standing, in the AMERICANA CORRIDORS, The GRACIOUS LIVING WING and the 1914 GARAGE! This remarkable collection, *valued at over a million dollars,* represents almost *every facet of American life!!* Make a note; NO TICKETS SOLD AFTER 4 P.M.!

825 N.E. OCEAN BLVD. —STUART, FL   (561) 225-1961
OPEN DAILY 1-5   ADMISSION

SOUTH FLORIDA SCIENCE MUSEUM

Heavens! What a WONDERFUL PLACE!! The SOUTH FLORIDA SCIENCE MUSEUM in *Dreher Park* has a variety of exhibits and programs for all ages... from archaeology to marine biology to space science!! The ALDRIN PLANETARIUM features a *special show* at 3 p.m daily except Monday, and YOU'LL SEE STARS at the GIBSON OBSERVATORY'S *Friday night viewing* of all heavens, weather permitting, of course.

ON DREHER TRAIL AT 1141 SUMMIT BLVD. — WEST PALM BEACH., FL
OPEN DAILY 10-5 FRI. TILL 10   ADMISSION   (561) 832-1988

NORTON GALLERY OF ART ELEGANCE

Art Lovers, you do not want to miss this!! A day would hardly be enough time to discover all the TREASURES!! This is one of the NATION'S MOST OUTSTANDING LARGE MUSEUMS!!! Paintings by CEZANNE, MATISSE, RENOIR and *others equally noted.* The CHARLES 1600's PORCELAIN COLLECTION is absolutely STUNNING!! There is a JADE COLLECTION *circa 1662...* and NETSUKE MINIATURE SCULPTURES from the *16th Century...*plus ARCHAIC TOMB JADES dating from *1500 BC to 500 BC.* That's reaching back some!! *Do study* the MOUNTAIN CARVING from 1600's. Carved in AMBER, it has *everything on a mountain from the natural things to cliffs to monks climbing with their staffs.* It is MAG-NI-FI-CENT!!! The permanents collections include paintings from the *French and American Schools* and sculpture? Just visit the beautifully landscaped PATIO GARDENS and SEE the *sculpture!!*

1451 S. OLIVE AVE. — WEST PALM BEACH, FL   (561) 832-5194
OPEN TUES-SAT 10-5 SUN 1-5   ADMISSION — DONATION

FORT LAUDERDALE HISTORICAL MUSEUM

History buffs will have their plate full... It takes you *'way back* into the early 1800's, with artifacts from BROWARD COUNTY'S *beginnings* right on up to the *present!!* There's a 1500-volume LIBRARY here if you want to do some research. One exhibit contains *beautiful men's and women's* FORMAL ATTIRE, children's and INDIAN clothing! And oh, there's a COLLECTION OF BELLS like you've never seen — all kinds of bells!! There's DEPRESSION GLASS — if you've never seen it, here's your chance! Another exhibit is a MINIATURE REPLICA OF OLD FORT

LAUDERDALE, *the fort which gave the city its name!* The Historical Museum is on the same grounds with the King-Cromarty House and Old Schoolhouse, on the New River.

219 S.W. 2ND AVE. — FT. LAUDERDALE, FL   OPEN (954) 463-4431
OPEN TUES.-FRI. 10-4   ADMISSION

UDT-SEAL MUSEUM — A LIVING TRIBUTE

Cloaked in secrecy, they took to the seas in World War II to become the UNIQUE UNDERWATER WARRIORS of the U.S. Navy! We know them as FROGMEN — those members of the *Underwater Demolition Teams*. From this *elite group* were drawn the SEALS: Sea Air Land Commandos, created in 1962!! The UDT-SEAL MUSEUM, located in Pepper Beach Park, contains the *actual equipment* used by these exceptional fighting men: their WEAPONS, DIVING GEAR, DEMOLITION EQUIPMENT — even a MIDGET SUBMARINE!! *Their deeds of valor* have earned them THREE MEDALS OF HONOR — our nation's HIGHEST HONOR. *They were "born" and trained* right there at PEPPER BEACH and you'll see VIDEO'S of that training as well as *actual operations*. Exciting? You bet! *Don't miss this!*

A1A (N. BEACH CAUSEWAY) — FT. PIERCE, FL PEPPER PARK
OPEN WED.-SUN. 10-4   ADMISSION   (772) 595-5845

BOCA RATON TOWN HALL 1927 &
COUNT deHOERNLE PAVILION 1930

The brilliant Addison Mizner designed townhall in Mediterranean Revival Style. Wood, brass hardware and decorative *ironwork* are throughout. Structure is topped by a gilded gold dome. Interior rooms are gracious with pecky cypress ceiling, original tile and shiny hardwood flooring. A garage houses "OLD BETSY", a 1926 La France fire engine (shiny & operative)!! Old crafted cabinets display historic Mizner artifacts — furniture and the old bank vault all have stories behind them. Historical Society also operates Count deHoernle Pavilion which goes by the more "plebian" title of *FEC Railroad Depot*. It too is Mediterranean Revival Style... a collection of several "cars" are on permanent display. Folks love snapping pics beside these old ironhorses. They include a 1930 Baldwin steam locomotive, a "64" Seaboard Caboose, 2 stainless steel 85 ft. cars, a lounge car and a diner of "50"'s vintage! Historical Society sponsors tours of old world BOCA RATON RESORT & CLUB. Tours of the sensational luxury palace are worth the $ $ $ — the only way you'll ever see it — this is not a "walk-in" place!!

BOCA RATON, FL TOWN HALL 71 NORTH
FEDERAL HWY (NO. OF PALMETTO PK RD)   (561) 395-6766
FEC RAIL DEPOT 747 S. DIXIE HWY.
(BETWEEN PALMETTO PK RD & CAMINO REAL)
TOWN HALL OPEN DAILY MON-FRI 9-5   FREE
SAT 1-4
RAIL DEPOT OPEN BY APPOINTMENT

AN 85,000 SQUARE FOOT "USEUM"

For starters (outside) the museum is a 52 ft. tall GREAT GRAVITY CLOCK. It is Florida's *largest kinetic energy sculpture*...It tells time by rolling balls moved by weights, pendulums and other "gadgets". Interior exhibit (areas 7) are stunningly showcased at MUSEUM OF DISCOVERY AND SCIENCE!!! *You* make it all happen. There are wheels to turn, buttons to push, levers to crank. I had to be "drug away" from Kalidescope displays where I waved big wands and magically created colors and symphonic sounds! Florida Ecoscapes is bi-level eco-mountain showing 8 native habitats — In the reef tank I made friends with "Homer", a bumblebee Grouper. His species can grow to 12 ft or 1,000 lbs. and is able to change sex. Space Base (5,500 sq. ft) simulations and experiments are interactive and p-o-p-u-l-a-r! The 7 exhibits are: FL EcoScapes, Space Base, KidScience, Choose Health, No Place Like Home, Sound and Traveling *Exhibit Hall*. This last one featured Giants of the Deep. Robot creatures were 10 ft. high to 27 ft. long. Orcas, Whales, Shark, Dolphin and Giant Squid. All were built from aluminum and steel and computer controlled even to the whales plaintive songs!!! Yep, there's more — BLOCKBUSTER IMAX THEATER! A rare type of cinema. Imax is short for "image maximum". Imax Theater combines special film technology, 60 ft. high by 80 ft. wide 5-story picture screen, a 14,000 watt, 6 channel, 4 way. 42-speaker sound system — Holy Cow, B-u-c-k-l-e U-p!!!

FT. LAUDERDALE FL 401 S.W. 2ND ST.   (954) 467-6637
OPEN MON.-FRI. 10-5 SAT. 10-8:30 P.M. SUN. 12-5   ADMISSION

YESTERYEAR VILLAGE

If you know what the following terms mean you're a purty smart number or else long-lived! Wash log, ash hopper, pitcher pump, hoop, gallberry bush? As you stroll the streets of this tiny hamlet you'll see why these items were so important to townfolks who lived in past centuries. In (30) RESTORED STRUCTURES you see weavers broom makers quilters and other artisans work their crafts. Outstanding buildings are the 1893 Red Level Church from Crystal River, 1936 Loxahatchee Groves Schoolhouse, 2-story 1900's Riddle Home & Lake Worth "L" Street House. An 1858 replica of HAILE PLANTATION home houses the Bink Glisson History Museum (lots of artifacts). Veteran's Home displays Civil & Indian War relics & documents— World War II Museum boasts many uniforms & era equipment. Scope out "Ole" General Store — buy food or antiques. In Blacksmith Shop workers exhibit a vanishing craft — Wait, there's more — Wood shop, Texaco Station, Lantana Bridge Tender's Home, Post Office, Printing Press, Flywheel engines, CALABOOSE & too much more to list!!! Village is in South FL Fairgrounds (130) acres, so many events, on-going year round.

WEST PALM BEACH FL OFF SOUTHERN BL   (561) 795-3110
1.5 MI WEST OF FL TURNPIKE   OPEN TUES.-SUN. 11-5   ADMISSION

THE GOLD BUG 2 TREASURE MUSEUMS

A 6,000 square foot museum exhibits bullion, coins and treasure from wrecks of the Spanish plate fleet sunk in 1715. Recent recoveries from the ocean floor include gold chains, jewelry and *solid gold bar!!* All treasure is processed on grounds and visitors may watch and speak with workers via a LABORATORY WINDOW!! Museum opened in "92" ...within 5 months 17,000 "gold-fevered folks" came through.

MEL FISHER'S TREASURE MUSEUM SEBASTIAN, FL
1320 US 1   OPEN MON.-SAT. 10-5; SUN. 12-5
ADMISSION   (772) 589-9875

You'll see *silver* and artifacts from the Spanish ships that went down in the hurricane of 1715. I was amazed at the beauty of sword hilts, buckles, rosary *figurines and ornaments.* McLARTY MUSEUM OPENED IN 1971.Today about 500 visitors a week stop by. There are cannon dioramas and historic displays. Indian tools and 18th century artifacts are also exhibited.

McLARTY MUSEUM SEBASTIAN INLET FL (2 MI SOUTH)   (772) 589-2147
HWY A1A OPEN 7 DAYS A WEEK 10-4:30   ADMISSION

TRAMP TRAMP TRAMP THE BOYS ARE MARCHING

I was s-p-e-e-c-h-l-e-s-s on viewing the WORLD'S LARGEST COLLECTION OF MINIATURE SOLDIERS & WEAPONRY! Exhibit takes up almost entire *second floor* of the museum...*Thousands* of tiny figures are all in (action poses) and detail is accurate to the rainbow colors on shields, face helmets and military pomp & dress. Weapons display include ancient to modern times. Military Historical Events are depicted from Roman Times up to Desert Storm with Norman Schwarzkopf!!! Below are only a *few of many* displays...

Goths Sack Rome 410 AD	Dark Ages
100 years War 1337	Attila The Hun Invades Rome
Sudan Cavalry 1890	Holy Land 1100
Knights Vs. Sarasens	William Normany Invades 1066
RAF Airfield 1940	Custer's Last Stand
Germany "Luftwaffe" 1914	Medieval Seige Artillery
Napoleanic Armies	British "RAJ" India 1890 Elizabethan Explorers
	(Elephants, Oxen) Ceremonial Parade

This *wondrous collection* is owned by one man, Edwin Reynolds and is worth coming a VERY LONG DISTANCE to see!!!

DELRAY BEACH FL 51 N. SWINTON AVE   (561) 243-7922
OLD SCHOOL SQUARE - CORNELL MUSEUM
OPEN TUES-SAT. 11-4   SUN 1-4   FREE

LOXAHATCHEE HISTORICAL MUSEUM

Museum of a (large) CRACKER STYLE building on 35 acres overlooking *Turtle Creek* — Loxahatchee is Indian for Turtle Creek or River. Permanent exhibits include Fossil Seashell Collection. Brightly colored

Seminole Indian Clothing, Early Railroad Artifacts, Trapper Nelson memorabilia, and early Jupiter photographs. *Changing Galleries* have rotating exhibits throughout the year — I saw a wonderful QUILT SHOW and demonstration one spring! The Historical Society operates 2 satellite museums that I'd go the "extra mile" to tour. They are JUPITER INLET LIGHTHOUSE and DUBOIS PIONEER HOME!!

JUPITER FL BURT REYNOLDS PARK   805 US 1 NORTH   (561) 747-6639
OPEN TUES-FRI 10-4   WEEKENDS 1-4   ADMISSION

Nature Centers

TOSOHATCHEE STATE RESERVE

Primitive! Beautiful! Unique! That's TOSOHATCHEE STATE RESERVE — *all 28,000 acres of it!* Woodlands and wetlands *abound* in this marvelous conservation area stretching for *19 miles* along the St. John's River. Marshes supply food for WADING and SHORE BIRDS — plus *migrating water fowl* in winter. Wooded uplands are home to WHITE-TAILED DEER, BOBCATS, GRAY FOX, TURKEYS — even hawks, owls and all kinds of songbirds. There's HISTORY, too, at TOSOHATCHEE RANCH HOUSE built in 1916 at the site of the *Second Seminole War.* There are *walking trails,* a *15-mile scenic drive, horseback riding and limited campsites.* S-U-P-E-R B-I-K-I-N-G because of forest canopy!!!

CHRISTMAS, FL — ON TAYLOR CREEK RD.   (352) 732-1255   FREE
4 MILES SOUTH OF FLORIDA 50   OPEN 8 A.M.-SUNSET YEAR 'ROUND

"POSSUM" LONG NATURE CENTER AN OASIS

This *'Possum* walked on TWO legs and he LOVED NATURE!! He was the late *Charles W. Long, Professor of Agriculture and Martin County High School Coach.* The Martin County Audubon Society purchased some 5 acres of *"Possum's" old homestead and nursery,* creating a *"quiet sanctuary"* for nature-lovers of every age!! Here you'll find many native and exotic plants growing wild — and you might even see some of the *beautiful birds and furry fauna* which have made this peaceful spot their home! You can "follow your nose" on your own through this *semi-jungle parkland,* or take a *guided tour.* Tours are conducted at 10 a.m. Mondays and Thursday, Saturdays by appointment.

HIBISCUS AVE. — STUART, FL   (561) 288-2637
OPEN — DAILY   ADMISSION — FREE

BARLEY BARBER SWAMP — ANCIENT WILDERNESS

Millions of years old!!! ANCIENT CYPRESS TRESS, *coffee-brown water* and a whole VARIETY of PLANT AND ANIMAL LIFE make Barley Barber Swamp *unique!* A BOARDWALK some *5800 feet long* takes you through this 400-acre preserve, with *33 numbered stations at points of interest along the way.* If you're lucky, you may see WOOD STORKS or BALD EAGLES as you stroll along. *Both are endangered species.* Other critters to watch for are RIVER OTTERS, DEER and RACCOONS!

Located just NORTH of Port Mayaca and the ICW. Visits are by RESER-VATION ONLY, *so call ahead for a date and time as well as specific directions on how to get here.*

INDIANTOWN FL - MARTIN FPL PLANT   (800) 552-8440 (561) 694-3646
OPEN -6 DAYS A WEEK - 2 DAILY TOURS   (800) 257-9267

GUMBO LIMBO NATURE CENTER
LIVING NATURAL HISTORY

There's a LOT TO SEE on these 15 acres! AT the ENVIRONMENTAL CENTER be sure to see the collection of *beautiful* BUTTERFLIES—hundreds of 'em!! And there are SPIDERS, too...*all kinds!* In yet another collection, *every kind of* SEASHELL *found on the S.E. Florida coast can be seen!!* There's a TURTLE POOL full of BABY LOGGERHEADS — just TWO INCHES LONG and *they come swimming right toward you* the minute you appear!! You'll see! The Center has a *big expansion program* underway — THREE new buildings with SALTWATER LINES direct from the ocean. Outside, *follow the 1628-foot GUMBO* LIMBO BOARDWALK through the COASTAL HAMMOCK! This is a *West Indian type hammock* — very RARE in Florida!! There are 28 DIFFERENT SPECIES OF TREES and PLANTS here, but the SURPRISE in this forest is the GUMBO LIMBO TREE!!! This tree, with it's *red peeling bark and feathering green fronds* is *endangered* now but there are *many* here.

1801 N. OCEAN BLVD. —BOCA RATON, FL   (561) 338-1473
OPEN MON.-SAT. 9 A.M.-4 P.M. SUN 12-4   FREE

HUGH TAYLOR BIRCH

At the heart of Ft. Lauderdale's "concrete jungle" is an exquisite BEACH HAMMOCK JUNGLE of 180 acres!! This *remnant of native coastal dunes* contains humongous seagrape trees, ancient knarled oaks, majestic banyans and rare chocolate gumbo-limbo trees.Take a CANOPY 2-MILE DRIVE through the park or try the PAR COURSE, an outdoor exercise circuit spaced along a 2.2-mile path. There are 20 stations and equipment is sized for *adults and youngsters.* Birch is sandwiched between *Atlantic Ocean beach and the Intracoastal Waterway,* so as you munch out on the seawall boaters provide ever-changing scenery. An UNDERPASS avoids busy Hwy. A1A and leads to 2 miles of beaches. PADDLEBOAT and CANOE RENTALS are on a freshwater lagoon. A 20-min. dune trail is revealing and relaxing!!!

SUNRISE BLVD., RD. 838 FT. LAUDERDALE, FL   (954) 564-4521
OPEN DAILY 8-SUNSET   ADMISSION

FERN FOREST NATURE CENTER PRIMITIVE

Talk about WILDERNESS! You'll see it in this last portion of the HISTORIC CYPRESS CREEK FLOODWAY!! 254 WILD ACRES with *32 varieties of fern,* a tropical HARDWOOD HAMMOCK, *open prairie* and *cypress-maple swamp!!* There are THREE nature trails: CYPRESS CREEK TRAIL, a half-mile long, elevated BOARDWALK (wheelchair accessible); PRAIRIE OVERLOOK TRAIL, a mile-long exploration of the open prairie; and MAPLE WALK, *a primitive trail* through a red maple swamp which you should *avoid in hot weather.* An exhibit room offers *audio-visual displays* about the park and there's a FREE *guided nature walk* every Sat. & Sun. at 2 p.m. A limited number of picnic tables are located north of the car park which has 98 spaces, 4 handicapped.

201 LYONS RD., SO. POMPANO BEACH, FL   (954) 970-0150
OPEN DAILY 9-5   FREE

EVERGLADES HOLIDAY PARK & CAMPGROUND

This place is HUMONGOUS!!! Some 4000 SQUARE MILES of *naturally beautiful* EVERGLADES! You'll need at least a DAY to enjoy it all, believe me!! Take a ride on Florida's BIGGEST AIR BOAT! Tours run *continuously* EVERY DAY 9-5! A *professional tour guide* explains all about this fabulous WONDERLAND!! Take in the WILDLIFE ANIMAL EXHIBIT — *gray fox, 'coons,* BOBCAT and a rare FLORIDA PANTHER, among others. Watch as MAN WRESTLES ALLIGATOR!! Wow! (DON'T FORGET YOUR CAMERA!) There's FISHING and HUNTING *(licenses available at the park)* and BOAT RENTALS. CAMPERS, *this is for you!!!* 100 RV spaces with full or partial hookups, plus *gas, laundry facilities* and *convenience store* with *ice and groceries 24 hours a day!* Tent camping is also available. Showers and restrooms are handy. Make a note: Park admission is FREE; however, there's a charge for EACH ACTIVITY including *picnic tables.*

21940 GRIFFIN RD.—FT. LAUDERDALE, FL   (954) 434-8111
OPEN—DAILY 9-5   ADMISSION

HOBE SOUND N.W.R.

The "sound" is a long (5 mi.) broad waterway separating JUPITER ISLAND from the mainland. Geography is *unusual* — on west shore are very high sugar-sand dune systems topped by pine scrub forest while on east shore is a 3 1/2 mile glittering beach! This is a 968 acre national Wildlife Refuge... It is probably America's most productive SEA TURTLE NESTING AREA for the humongous leatherback, green and loggerhead sea turtle creatures. On good years over 100,000 hatchlings are produced on the refuge's 3.5 mile beachfront! Take time to walk SAND PINE SCRUB NATURE TRAIL. where are "gentleman" scrub jay, fox, deer and other small animals. Hobe Sound Nature Center operates an *interpretive museum* open to the public...there are neat exhibits to touch and watch. Nearby waters of Jupiter Narrows are often visited by the docile 1,800 pound seacows. Refuge is accessible by car or boat.

HOBE SOUND FL (1 MI) SOUTH ON US 1   (772) 546-6141
OPEN DAILY DAYLIGHT HOURS   FREE

Parks With Pizazz

WICKHAM PARK — GREAT ESCAPE IN THE CITY
Wanna have a PICNIC? *Go camping?* Gather your gear and head for

Melbourne's WICKHAM PARK!! Located just *one mile* west of U.S. 1 on Parkway Drive, this 490-acre recreational park is IT!!! There are *pavilions* for family or group picnics, *two* lakes for swimming, *plus* archery and gun ranges for eagle eyes! The 88 campsites are equipped with *all* the necessaries: water, electricity, grills and tables. Bathhouses, too, with showers and lavs.

PARKWAY DRIVE — MELBOURNE, FL   (321) 255-4307
OPEN DAILY, 7 A.M. 'TIL DARK   ADMISSION

SEBASTIAN INLET

Moodiest inlet on the east coast. Some days wild and furious; others, like a pussycat. The park's 576 acres are *exceptionally gorgeous* because it lies between the Indian River and Atlantic Ocean. EVERYWHERE are dunes, lagoons, coves, jetties and glinting sandspits! *Camping is riverside* on both north and south side. A TOWERING BRIDGE spans strong inlet currents and below on "catwalks" are scores of fish poles attached to "generous folks" engaged in fish-feeding! I netted a 47-lb. DRUM here (in 1974)! You'll find boat ramps and 3 MILES OF OCEANFRONT for frolicking, surfing or skin and scuba diving. On grounds is McLARTY MUSEUM displaying exhibits and some treasure from the SPANISH GOLD FLEET wrecked offshore in 1715!!!

5 MI. NORTH ON A1A —WABASSO, FL   (321) 984-4852
OPEN—DAILY 8 SUNSET   ADMISSION

THE SAVANNAS

In 1963 canals were cleared and island created to give public access to *5 miles of savanna wilderness water marshes.*Today a 550-acre secluded CAMPGROUND nestles at the entrance to these silent mysterious savannas!! CANOE RENTALS get you to the "special spots" and PETTING ZOO with goats, piggies, rabbits, chicks and ponies keeps the little ones amused. Lots of FOOTBRIDGES criss-cross lily pad canals and carrot trees, and scrub oak adorn the median strips. Boat Ramps are good and 7 1/2 horse motors are the rule. Road 712 East dead-ends into Road 707 North. It is a marvy SCENIC RIVER DRIVE. It toodles north about 10 miles and brings your blood pressure down 10 points!! SAVANNAS has camping and day use fees. Neat COUNTY park!!

4 MI. SOUTH OFF U.S. 1, EAST ON RD. 712, FT. PIERCE, FL   800-789-5776
OPEN — DAILY 8 A.M.-SUNDOWN   ADMISSION   (772) 468-3985

PEPPER BEACH PARK — LOTS TO DO

WHAT A PLACE!!! *Two thousand feet of sandy beach on the sparkling blue Atlantic,* PEPPER BEACH PARK is *kind of unique!!!* Tennis courts were added in 1987 and there are *excellent facilities* here: *pavilions* in the *picnic area,* shelters, DUNE OVERWALKS, FISHING *(bring your gear!),* showers and restrooms, plus *facilities for the handicapped.* In addition, there's a *local history museum* which highlights the AIS INDIANS, the 1715 SPANISH SILVER FLEET disaster (all that *treasure!),* the SEMINOLE WARS and the LOST AMERICAN GOLD PAYROLL!!! You'll also find the UDT-SEAL MUSEUM here (see "Museums"). There's free parking for 400 or more cars.

S. A1A (N. BEACH CAUSEWAY) — FT. PIERCE, FL
OPEN DAWN TO DUSK

JONATHAN DICKINSON

HOBE MOUNTAIN'S observation tower overlooks part of the park's 10,284 acres. A BIKE PATH meanders besides old railroad tracks. *Loxahatchee River* is the gem in this setting and is best seen by canoe. Not to worry... Plenty of *canoe rentals.* Scores of "oxbows" lend excitement to your water journey and one "Senator Cypress" is awesome!! If canoes aren't your bag, go in comfort on the LOXAHATCHEE QUEEN CRUISE. It goes to "Trapper Nelson Site." It is a narrated tour. There are 3 nature treks. One follows the river, another leads to Kitching Creek and one to Hobe Mountain. Wanna camp? Do it. Rent a cabin? Sure can! Nearby on Jupiter Island is BLOWING ROCKS PRESERVE where mighty ocean waves duel with gigantic rock forms!!! Do visit!

HOBE SOUND FL U.S. 1-16450 S.E. FEDERAL HWY.   ADMISSION
OPEN — DAILY 8 A.M.-SUNSET   BOAT TOURS (561) 746-1466
                                   PARK (772) 546-2771

PHIPPS PARK — CAMPING BY THE BIG DITCH

This bee-u-tiful park is *smack-dab* on the banks of the ST. LUCIE CANAL — just a HOOT AND A HOLLER from the LOCKS!!! There are campsites for self-contained RV's — *no water, sewer or electrical hookups here,* through you can fill your water tank at the *"community" faucet!* Lots of GREEN ACRES here, *some 127 of 'em, with 50 developed.* And HIKING TRAILS — *you can go clear to the Florida turnpike* if your "boots are made for walkin'." There are PICNIC AREAS here for your enjoyment, there are *no food concessions* here — and leave BOW-WOW or KITTY-KAT at home "cuz PETS aren't welcome! *No reservations,* either — *first come, first served!!!*

2175 S.W. LOCKS RD. —STUART, FL   (772) 287-6565
OPEN 6 A.M. - 7:30 P.M.   ADMISSION

JOHN PRINCE PARK — IN THE HEART OF THE CITY

Something for EVERYONE here! Over 1,000 ACRES on beautiful LAKE OSBORNE in the *heart of Lake Worth.* PICNIC AREAS — bring your favorite munchin's...a GOLF DRIVING RANGE, RECREATION AREA, NATURE TRAIL, BIKING... plus CAMPING, FISHING, CANOE & SAILBOARD RENTALS. John Prince Park is also the site of the RAYMOND F. KRAVIS CENTER for the PERFORMING ARTS if you want to add a little culture to your life!   SEE MAP PG. 59

4300 S. CONGRESS — LAKE WORTH, FL   (561) 582-7992 CAMP
OPEN—SUNRISE-SUNSET   ADMISSION — FREE
PARK INFO (561) 966-6600   BOAT RENT (561) 964-0178

FT. PIERCE INLET   STATE REC AREA

A grand slice of oceanfront. More enjoyable because of a *sea inlet.* Park is popular for swimming and SURFING!! Upland section are dunes and hammocks. Low area is mangrove. Try Dynamite Point for "birding"! Craft are always zooming in & out of inlet. Total acreage is 340... You'll find bathhouses walk trails and YOUTH CAMPING. I enjoy the *jetty* on (southside) as it has a wide paved top for ambling. ...this way you get to talk with the fisherfolks and they get to tell you LIES!!!

FT. PIERCE FL	NORTH BEACH CAUSEWAY	(772) 468-3985
2200 N. BEACH B.	OPEN DAILY 8-SUNSET	ADMISSION

GET HEALTHY   GET CULTURED

Pack your "toys"...bikes, rollerblades or skates, tennis racquet, racquetballs & jog shoes —OR— your *sittin' & watchin' cushion!* RIVERSIDE PARK is 54 acres of relaxing green bliss on INDIAN RIVER... paved paths entice bikers & skaters. You may picnic or grill goodies or watch couples argue about how to launch their craft down the BOAT RAMP!! A wee 8-acre-island (Memorial Park) pokes out into Indian River — just cross footbridge and explore! Now, comes C-U-L-TR-U-R-E. On the same grounds is CENTER FOR THE ARTS. It is a $2 million structure built in 1986 having 34,000 square feet within. Variety, rotating exhibits and careful selections are keys to the art center success. You'll admire permanent *displays of Sculpture and paintings*...or "special showings" of Baroque Goldsmiths and Jewelers Art from Hungary. A favorite event is the annual COLLECTOR's CHOICE EXHIBIT which displays elegant works of Picasso, Rembrandt, Marsh and modern artists!!

VERO BEACH FL RIVERSIDE PARK ON ORCHID ISLAND
(EAST SIDE 17TH ST. BRIDGE)   OPEN DAILY
ART CENTER 3001 RIVERSIDE PARK DR   (772) 231-0707
OPEN DAILY 10-4:30 THURS 10-8
SUMMER (MAY-SEPT) TUES-SAT 10-4:30 SUN 1-4:30
THURS 10-8 CLOSED MONDAY   FREE

Scenic Drives

PRETTY TROPICAL TRAIL...IT HAS ANOTHER NAME

Take time for a restful, scenic drive with a SURPRISE AT THE END! Just south of Rt. 520, Rd. 3 meanders down the Merritt Island Peninsula from some 15 1/2 miles... through cypress trees and sawgrass, homes tucked here and there. To the east, the Banana River gets *closer and closer and* CLOSER!!! You may want to pause at the M.I. POTTERY WORKS, *a fixture since 1937.* Just below *Mather's Bridge,* Rt. 404, the road narrows, bordered now by both the Banana and Indian Rivers. Continue on past *mango groves* and large homes with *fine old trees* arching over the road. Just beyond, a first road goes to *land's end* and that's the surprise: a 100-FOOT LONG GREEN DRAGON which guards the peninsula!!! *Wee hatchlings* have been added by its creator, Lewis VanDercar. It contains over 20 TONS of *concrete and steel!!* It's this *benevolent monster* which gave Tropical Trail its *other* name: DRAGON DRIVE!! Dragon seen only by BOAT!

MERRITT ISLAND, FL   OPEN DAILY   FREE

BLUFFS DRIVE

Begin at juncture of Road 712 and Road 707, 7 miles south of FT. PIERCE. GO NORTH on Rd. 707. A marvelous *3-story white mansion sits serenely on this crossroad* and indicates the treats in store! The narrow drive overlooks BLUFFS 15 to 30 feet high beside wide shallow INDIAN RIVER. Sweeping lawns are extensive with each yard displaying its own botanical creations. At points the road is a bit "roller coastery" and many docks tether dancing sailboats! Architectural mix includes a bit of ADOBE, SPANISH HACIENDA, SHAKE ROOF AND SALT BOX. NORTH SECTION of drive revels *older more classic style homes* with Gumbo Limbo trees, enormous rope cactus and perky flowers providing outdoor window dressing. Your scenic path winds up in OLD TIMEY downtown Ft. Pierce...Why not check out a few of the shops???

FT. PIERCE, FL   DIRECTIONS — ABOVE
OPEN — DAILY   FREE

JUPITER ISLAND TOUR

BOTANICAL GARDEN DRIVE would be a more apt name for this island for although it is home to the *international jet set,* their "palaces" are not visible. YOUR TREATS are the *incredible botanical gardens* sprouting from each private property. For many miles you can wonder at lush multi-green fern, Seaside Mahoe with yellow-crimson blooms and literally hundreds of tropical exotics. North of Rd. 707 is 3-mile HOBE SOUND NATIONAL WILDLIFE REFUGE where you may beach hike, fish, swim or photo. There is fine parking (but no other facilities). Jupiter drive is direct and the tendency is to accelerate...DON'T...*unmarked patrol cars* are most vigilant! At mid-island BLOWING ROCKS PRESERVE astounds visitors brave enough to walk atop bulwarks where furious seas crash shoreward spewing salty foam everywhere!! Hours are Daily 6 a.m.-5 p.m. Diving and fishing are allowed.

HOBE SOUND, FL — ST. LUCIE COUNTY, A1A
OPEN-DAILY   FREE

FLAGLER GOLDCOAST DRIVE YACHTS & MANSIONS

As a SCENIC ROAD, *Flagler Drive is hard to match!* Curving along the western shore of beautiful LAKE WORTH, you'll see *magnificent 150-foot* YACHTS out there and some of those *fabulous* PALM BEACH MANSIONS across the lake!! To the west, *modern high rise architecture...like* PHILLIPS POINT, a unique building ALL IN PINK *including the windows!!!* There are views of old SPANISH-STYLE structures with tile roofs...homes and condos with small BOTANICAL GARDENS in front! Larger shopping centers are interspersed along the way with lovely GREEN PARKS and *picturesque* ARCHED BRIDGES *spanning the lake.* Tootle over one or two blocks to the OLD SECTION where so many HISTORIC BUILDINGS *are being preserved...* on OLIVE and CLEMATIS Streets. Little green

PARKS *pop up everywhere here* with hugh *banyan tree groves!* Back on Flagler you'll want to visit historic ST. ANNE'S CATHOLIC CHURCH & SCHOOL *with its old architecture.* The drive extends 4 or 5 miles and you can WALK OR BIKE it if you want some exercise!!

FLAGLER DRIVE — WEST PALM BEACH, FL   OPEN DAILY   FREE

ESTATES OVERLOOKING THE ATLANTIC

And WHAT SIGHTS!! Bordering the *blue Atlantic,* South Ocean Boulevard, with its *seawalls* and WALK PATH is scenic on BOTH SIDES!! Tall PALMS *split the sky everywhere,* and on your right you'll begin to see some of the PALATIAL PALM BEACH MANSIONS!!! These are E-NOR-MOUS ESTATES... these homes of the *very wealthy. The grounds are so perfectly* MANICURED I betcha if a leaf or twig starts to fall, *a gardener is there to catch it before it hits the ground!!!* It's here you'll see the famous MAR-A-LAGO, *the magnificent estate* built by MARJORIE MERRI-WEATHER POST in 1927. *You can't miss* it with its MOORISH TOWER. Today, Mar-A-Lago is owned by Mister Donald Trump. As you drive along, you may see, far out to sea, some of the huge FREIGHTERS *on their way to the rest of the world! You can drive many miles along this scenic highway...*South Ocean Boulevard, another HIGHLIGHT of fabulous PALM BEACH!!!

PALM BEACH, FL — S. OCEAN BLVD.   OPEN—DAILY   FREE

NORTH NEW RIVER DRIVE — AN HISTORIC TOUR

Indian LEGEND tells us that the NEW RIVER was born during an AWESOME STORM, amid great THUNDERING, *a blazing flash of* LIGHT and the *trembling of the earth!!!* However it came to be, it's one of the OLDEST charted rivers in the NEW WORLD!!! This is a DEEP RIVER — 90 FEET in some spots! *No going aground here!* The drive along the NORTH FORK is *especially scenic* and well worth taking. Tarry awhile in COONEY HAMMOCK PARK at TARPON BEND. *There's history here,* for while it's a *serene and lovely spot* today, it's also the site of the Lewis Family's ORIGINAL HOMESTEAD, believed to have been *destroyed* by the SEMINOLES in the 1836 *massacre!!* This drive is right in downtown Fort Lauderdale at the lower end of S.E. 1st Avenue. Hang a left and you're there.

N. NEW RIVER DRIVE — FT. LAUDERDALE, FL   OPEN — DAILY   FREE

JUNGLE TRAIL   7 MILES

This seven mile *scenic corridor* overlooks river vistas, original orange groves and hide-away islands. In 1990 Jungle Trail was given the FLORI-DA TRUST AWARD FOR HISTORIC PRESERVATION!!! Donkeys years ago I cruised via sailboat this gorgeous passage... I've no boat any longer but am delighted that I can still be surrounded by the same natural beauty by driving the "trail" in my buggy. Hole-In-The-Wall Island, Pine Island and others are often filled with bird rookeries. You may observe their clackitting chatter and constant jostling for better nest space. Some unde-veloped upland islands have wild yellow cactus bloom (grapefruit) size with plants growing several feet high. West of your drivepath are the *"nar-*

rows" of the Intracoastal Waterway. This remote quiet waterway is popular with the "slow-motion" gentle SEACOWS! Trail has 2 parts (3 mi. south & 4 Mi. north) of Rd 510 — NEAT BICYCLING!!

WABASSO FL SOUTH OF RD 510 BRIDGE ON JUNGLE TR
OR OFF HWY A1A   HISTORICAL SOCIETY ON JUNGLE TRAIL
ON OLD WINTER BEACH RD   (561) 778-3435

Someplace Different

GILBERT'S BAR HOUSE OF REFUGE

Has a reassuring ring, doesn't it? Here's why! HOUSE OF REFUGE 1875 is the *only 1 of 9* such houses remaining which gave aid to *shipwrecked sailors. With its old LIGHTHOUSE, it perches on mammoth rocks* where 20 feet below Atlantic waves SMASH into crevices and pools creating new rock patterns. Camera shots are worth getting SEA-SPRAYED!!! Stop at the BOAT HOUSE with its early life-saving equipment and exhibits; tour the MAIN HOUSE furnished in late Victorian. It's the OLDEST STRUCTURE in the area and *well worth discovering for yourself!*

HUTCHINSON ISLAND, FL — ON RT A1A NEAR STUART   (561) 225-1875
OPEN — TUES.-SUN. 1-4 CLOSED MON.   ADMISSION

MERRITT ISLAND N.W.R. BIRDIES & BEASTIES GALORE

This SPACE AGE REFUGE was created at the time Kennedy Space Center was founded! MERRITT ISLAND NATIONAL WILDLIFE REFUGE lies under the great ATLANTIC FLYWAY, drawing over *200,000* feathered visitors during migration!!! Some stay for the winter and many are year-rounders. All in all, some *300 species* have been sighted by birdwatchers. Look for the colorful ROSEATE SPOONBILL among others! 'Course, birds aren't the only critters to be seen. The refuge is home to many Florida animals — armadillos, 'coons, bunnies, 'gators and even BOBCATS!! There are *two hikin trails:* OAK HAMMOCK and MAX HOECK CREEK, plus *two car drives* from which you might catch a peek of the furry fauna...and surely the feathered fellas. 'Specially in *early morning* or *late afternoon.* Get detailed info at Refuge Headquarters, 5 1/2 miles east of Indian River on Rd. 402.

TITUSVILLE, FL   (321) 861-0667
OPEN — DAYS ONLY   FREE

SPACEPORT, U.S.A. — OUT OF THIS WORLD

"Fly me to the moon..." Can't do that, but once you've toured SPACE-PORT, U.S.A., you'll kind of get the *feeling* you WERE THERE! It all begins at the VISITORS' CENTER. *Nifty exhibits:* a Lunar Rover on a simulated moonscape, MOON ROCKS, a *Viking Spacecraft* on a *Martian landscape and more!!!* So many things to see, all *historic* and *fascinating.*

Like the IMAX THEATER with its 5 1/2-story high Vehicle Assembly Building (you can see it for miles!) and Cape Canaveral Air Force Station. Visit the LUNCH PAD and the ORBIT CAFETERIA. From Titusville, take NASA Parkway (SR 405) to Merritt Island. Look for the Visitors' Center on right.

MERRITT ISLAND, FL   (321) 449-4444
OPEN — DAILY 8-4   ADMISSION

ANNE KOLB NATURE CENTER — WEST LAKE PARK

Extensive exhibit hall is gateway to 1500 acre West Lake Park bordering (3 miles) of INTRACOASTAL WATERWAY!!! Nature Center occupies a 20 acre site. It has static & interactive displays plus a 4000 gallon salt-water aquarium. ECO-ROOM has collections games & "hands-on" displays. Outside you climb the (68 ft) observation tower with views "clear to China." There are several trails . . . . Longest (2.3 mi). Fish?? Sure, on 870 ft pier. Most popular is a narrated 40 min BOAT TOUR. There are r-e-n-t-a-l boats, canoes & kayaks . . . . A 5000 ft bike path wears-out "wee-folk"! You may want to rent the 6060 sq ft Assembly Building for a public or private "Do"----More fun yet, visit when a festival or event is happening in the 4600 sq ft CENTRAL PATIO!!!

HOLLYWOOD FL 751 SHERIDAN ST
OPEN-DAILY   (954) 926-2480

PORT MAYACA LOCKS ON THE SHORE OF THE BIG WATER

This is the GATEWAY to LAKE OKEECHOBEE — the second-largest lake in the continental U.S.!!! It's not big — it's HUGE! Twenty-seven miles across! At PORT MAYACA, you'll have a great view of the lake. You'll also see ALL KINDS OF BOATS locking through! The locks are operated and maintained by the U.S. Army Corps of Engineers. You can park by the Corps Office and the LOCKMASTER will be glad to show you around (traffic permitting). Or, you can DRIVE ALONG THE TOP OF THE DIKE. Look for GATORS basking on top of the water and on the banks!!! This is a short side trip from Stuart.

RD. 76 — PORT MAYACA, FL
OPEN 6 A.M. - 10 P.M.   FREE

JUPITER LIGHTHOUSE — A TOWER OF STRENGTH

Imagine being 105 feet aboveground in awesome HURRICANE WINDS!!! That's what happened in 1928 to 16-year-old FRANKLIN SEABROOK, son of Capt. Charles Seabrook, Keeper of Jupiter Lighthouse. When the power failed in the worst hurricane of the young century, Capt. Seabrook installed the ORIGINAL MINERAL LAMPS, but due to a severely injured hand, he could not turn the MANTLE. That's when his son took over! Jupiter Light, with its 880,000 CANDLEPOWER has been a beacon of hope to mariners since 1860 and can be seen for 18 miles out to sea. Only twice has it been darkened: during the Civil War and briefly during that *1928 hurricane.* Today, Jupiter Light is manned by U.S. Coast Guardsmen. It has seen MANY CHANGES in its *colorful lifespan* — if ONLY it could TALK!!

LIGHTHOUSE PARK, CAPT. ARMOUR WAY — JUPITER, FL   ADMISSION
OPEN SUN. 1-4   (561) 747-8380

SPANISH RIVER PARK — A BEAUTY

This is one expansive PARK!! Bordered by the *Atlantic on the east, the Intracoastal Waterway to the west,* the park takes its name from the old SPANISH RIVER. The river was *rechanneled to become part of the ICW, but remnants of the original streambed* can still be seen in the park. This is really a NEAT place, with *plenty of parking* in TWO BIG LOTS. There are PICNIC AREAS equipped with *grills, tables and restrooms* for FAMILY outings, plus PAVILIONS for *large group picnics!* (By reservation only. Call (407) 393-7811.) The HIGHLIGHT of Spanish River Park is its BOTANICAL GARDEN with OLD SPECIES OF FLORIDA TREES that are *almost gone* elsewhere! There's a NATURE TRAIL and FOOTPATHS along the Intracoastal through *lush tropical foliage* so DENSE only *dappled sunlight* penetrates!! TUNNELS cross under A1A to *1 1/2 miles of oceanfront* for swimming. Lifeguards are stationed at intervals all along the nice sandy beach. Spanish River is a DAY USE ONLY PARK.

3001 N. OCEAN BLVD. (A1A) — BOCA RATON, FL   (561) 393-7977
OPEN — DAILY 8 A.M.-SUNDOWN   ADMISSION

ST. LUCIE LOCK, DAM & NATURE TRAIL
BOATS, BARGES, YACHTS

GREAT SPORT for *boat-watchers!!!* All sizes and descriptions go through busy St. Lucie Lock — *as many as 200 A DAY on a good weekend!!!* The lock lifts the boats as much as 15 FEET - like going through a *miniature* PANAMA CANAL! The lock-site has attractive park-like surroundings with a *children's playground* and some *25 campsites with full facilities.* Nearby is the ST. LUCIE NATURE TRAIL, a pleasant walk through a *variety of habitats* with several points of interest. If you look real sharp, you may see tracks or signs of the *various animals* which live here — or you might even catch a glimpse of 'em!

S.W. LOCKS RD (R 76) — STUART, FL   (561) 452-2121
OPEN — DAILY 6 A.M. - 7:30 P.M.   FREE

LOXAHATCHEE NATIONAL WILDLIFE REFUGE
BASS-N-GATOR COUNTRY

No PRESERVATIONS here!!! This is ALL-NATURAL OLD FLORIDA! Some *221 square miles* (over 200,000 ACRES) of *bee-u-tiful wildlife refuge,* with sawgrass, palmettos, cabbage palms, mangroves — and of course, WILDLIFE! GATORS, WATERFOWL, FURRY CRITTERS — they're here! Things to DO? Oh, my YES! AIRBOAT RIDES, BOAT RENTALS, WALK ROADS and *anglers,* 'TENSHUN! This is probably the FINEST BIG BASS FISHING AREA in the WORLD!! *Bring your own tack-*

le or rent it right there. Bait is available.

U.S. 441 (SR 7) — BOYNTON BEACH, FL   (561) 734-8303
OPEN — DAILY   ADMISSION

ELLIOTT KEY AND CORAL REEFS

It is 7 miles long; 7 miles from the mainland and traces of pineapple and key lime plantations still remain. Elliott has 68 boat slips, showers, free campgrounds and hike trails. It is part of BISCAYNE NATIONAL PARK'S 181,500 acres and 42 islands. Nearby REEFS grow 50 types of rainbow corals. *Spectacular branches* of ELKHORN AND STAGHORN CORAL can be seen. There are 18th century wrecks plus SANDS and BOCA CHITA KEYS for the curious!! This water-wonderworld can be enjoyed via GLASS-BOTTOMED TOUR BOATS as you o-o-oh and a-h-h-h at *fat sea turtles, pink coral and tropical fish!!!* 3 and 4 hour tours range in price. Special trips to scuba or snorkel are available. In 1986 30 professors from MARINE PARKS around the world were enchanted by stunning reef displays and marine life!!! Come and visit...that many experts can't be wrong!

15 MI. EAST — HOMESTEAD, FL   BISCAYNE NATIONAL PARK INFO
TOUR BOAT INFO (305) 230-1100   (305) 230-7275

THAR SHE BLOWS — BLOWING ROCKS PRESERVE

They aren't called BLOWING ROCKS for nothing! Water flumes slam into *coral rock ledges and cliffs* which you can STAND ATOP. Waves and foam seek rock holes to come spewing up, unexpectedly dampening visitors! Between "drenchings" peek 15 feet below and marvel at the cutting power of these mighty waters on the mile-long reef!!! BLOWING ROCKS PRESERVE is a private sanctuary of Nature Conservancy. Diving and snorkeling are allowed but is difficult in rough seas...calm days are great! Behind first dune line is a short nature walk prettied up by yucca, sea grapes, waving oat plumes (not pick) and hearty black-eyes Susans. For sheer POWER and BEAUTY Blowing Rocks Preserve is hard to beat!

A1A 2 MI. NORTH OF JUPITER INLET — JUPITER ISLAND, FL
OPEN — DAILY 6-5   (561) 575-2297

CITY PLACE

West Palm Beach exploded into 2001 with a DOWNTOWN 72 acre European type residential, shopping & cultural venue. Entire project overlooks an Italianate main plaza, grand staircases, & 186 jet fountain arching multicolored geysers skyward. 600 live/work lofts & townhouses surround this extravaganza!! MACY's is 1 of the 78 specialty stores & 10 dining shops bordering the plaza. The "SOUL" of City Place is — The Harriet — a 1920's church with a $6 million renovation now used as a cultural venue. It boasts 11,000 sq. ft., tiered mezzanine, a breath-tacular open truss pecky vaulted ceiling and original 5-sets of double entry cypress French doors!!! On an upper gallery is a 20 screen movie theater. I spent hours roaming about FAO Schwarz, a gourmet market and who can resist CHEESECAKE FACTORY...free parking for 3,300 cars is a nice touch...Don't forget to hop the trolley to CLEMATIS STREET DISTRICT (a more modest shop/dine area) but still a neat place to hang out. City Place will require plenty of "discovery time"----not to worry----just check into the 400 room hotel nearby on Okeechobee Bl.

WEST PALM BEACH, FL 700 S. ROSEMARY AVE (DOWNTOWN)
(561) 366-1000

PIER 66 — THE MAGIC NUMBER

If you want to see BOATS, this is THE-E-E PLACE!!! *Hundreds of 'em* are berthed here at Pier 66! HUGE YACHTS, sleek and elegant — if you don't see your *dream boat* in this *enormous marina,* well, you never will!! PIER 66 — marina and hotel — was inspired in 1954 by K.S. "BOOTS" ADAMS, retired president of Phillips Petroleum. (NOW you know the source of that magic number!) The resort covers 22 acres and for a SPECTACULAR VIEW, *day or night,* just go on up to the PIER TOP LOUNGE! The elevator will get you there in 66 SECONDS...and the *lounge rotates* in 66 MINUTES! so you'll have plenty of time to enjoy the view as well as your favorite libation!! This is a Fort Lauderdale LANDMARK — ashore and at sea!

2301 S.E. 17TH ST. CAUSEWAY — FT. LAUDERDALE, FL   FREE
OPEN — DAILY   (954) 525-6666

NEW RIVER TUNNEL — A FIRST IN FLORIDA

Wheee!! Just like NEW YORK CITY!!! This highway tunnel — named for HENRY A. KINNEY — is the ONLY ONE *in Florida!* It takes U.S. 1 some 45 FEET *beneath the New River!!!* It's a pretty PINK tunnel, brightly lighted! It open in 1960, replacing the old drawbridge with its *constant openings.* The BOAT TRAFFIC was darn near as heavy as the *stream of cars up on the highway!!*

U.S. 1 — FT. LAUDERDALE,FL   (DOWNTOWN)
OPEN — DAILY   FREE

BUTTERFLY WORLD — BEAUTY ON THE WING

It's a butterfly zoo — sans peanuts and popcorn!! There are *literally* THOUSANDS from *all over the world!* I'm not talking about specimens in cases — though you'll see those in the BUTTERFLY MUSEUM. But in the screened AVIARY GARDENS these beautiful *"flying flowers"* are ALIVE, flitting from blossom to blossom!! It's an ENCHANTING sight! In the BREEDING LAB, you'll see the *life cycle of the butterfly* from the moment it *hatches* to the day it GETS ITS WINGS!! If you haven't heard of Butterfly World before — it's NEW and a *major part* of the effort to save the now *endangered butterfly!!* It's located in TRADEWINDS PARK.

3600 W. SAMPLE RD. —COCONUT CREEK, FL   (954) 977-4400
OPEN — DAILY 9-5, SUN. 1-5   ADMISSION

CORAL CASTLE

Love carved in STONE!! A Latvian jilted by his dreamgirl the night before his wedding came to the States in 1913 to mend a broken heart. Ed Leedskalnin (All 5 feet, 100 pounds of him) built a CASTLE to his lost love. Some coral rocks are 36 tons. There is a 5000-lb. love table in the shape of a heart. Sit in the coral chairs (they rock) and admire a table in the shape of Florida, with scooped out fingerbowl (Lake Okeechobee) in the center. There is a THRONE and a 9-ton GATE easily pushed open. Ed worked in the *dead of night* and kept secret his method for moving the weighty limestone rocks. Lay in the CONTOUR CHAIRS (Facing east and west) for suntanning. See the 25-ft. telescope (30 tons). There are many more carvings. I was intrigued by the upper room personal quarters Leedskalnin lived in... very SPARTAN...note his bed on ceiling pulleys. When asked how he created his works Ed would say, "I know the secret of the pyramids"!!

U.S. ! AT 286TH ST., S.W. — HOMESTEAD, FL   (305) 248-6345
OPEN — DAILY 9-9   ADMISSION

UNCAGED METROZOO

Top 10 rating...here's why...No bars,no cages, It's *untamed, uninhibited, unusual.* The animals ROAR, SPLASH, LEAP, SWING, SNAP, HISS, SCRRCH, HOP and have a howling good time! A monorail whisks you through the 300-acre park (740 acres total). Kuddly koalas are everyone's favorite. African elephants cavort in their own pool and TOSHI, the Japanese black rhino has 2 girlfriends, CORA and LULU. A *free-flight aviary* for exotic birds resembles a rain forest. Kids will love the "petting zoo" complete with elephant rides!! I think Metrozoo is a true ADVENTURE worth tripping all the way from Jacksonville to Miami for!!!

12400 S.W. 152ND ST. — MIAMI, FL
(CORAL REEF DR. WEST OF FLORIDA TURNPIKE EXIT)   (305) 251-0403
OPEN 10-5:30 — LAST TICKET 4 P.M.   ADMISSION

CITY SLICKERS OASIS

Try "chilling out" in cool refreshing waters of West lake and grabbing el sol's rays on a white sandy beach. SNYDER PARK is a 92 acre reserve smackdab in the heart of Ft. Lauderdale! The 2 lakes provide SWIMMING & fishing. A *sub-tropical setting* includes peeling Gumbo-Limbos, Live Oaks adorned with airplants and other exotics. Raccoon, bunnies and silly opossums are usually overhead. Lunch shelters look out on the lakes — a most helpful feature is a *Handicapped Swim Ramp.* Anglers have a fishing pier, walkers enjoy nature Trails and there are BOAT RENTALS! The city bought this land in 1966 for a mere $375,000 — today's price tag would be a million-billion dollars!

FT. LAUDERDALE FL   3299 S.W. 4TH AVE.   (954) 761-5346
                           CITY PARKS & REC (954) 468-1585
OPEN — DAILY   ADMISSION

HARBOR BRANCH OCEANOGRAPHIC INSTITUTION

It is 1 of 3 in the country and in the same "big 1 league" as Wood's Hole in Massachusetts or Scripps in California! H.B. has its own deep water canal off Indian River. It employs *200 persons* with 1 in 6 holding a doctorate degree! About 1,000 folks a month take the tour. It is by tram or bus, 1 1/2 hours and offers an *inside view* of Harbor Branch's work which is acquaculture, ocean engineering, marine science and biomed marine study. If not out on a project you'll see (not tour) their 170 foot, 168 foot and 100 foot *research vessels*. SUBMERSIBLES are key tools at the center...They descend 3,000 ft. You may hop into a full-scale mock up of a JOHNSON SEA LINK SUBMERSIBLE. H.B. covers 500 acres.

FT. PIERCE FL (HALFWAY TO VERO FL)   (772) 465-2400
5600 US HWY 1 NORTH   TOURS 10, 12, 2 MON-SAT
OPEN TOURS 10, 12, 2 MON-SAT   ADMISSION

BATHTUB BEACH

A sort of "ocean washpan" 3 ft. deep which is hugged by a 1 mile long, 85 acre *fragile REEF* and 1,080 foot sandy beach. The barrier reef enclosing "bathtub cove" is the engineering project of tens of thousands of worms 3/4 of an inch long. They've built *sand-tubes* evolving into a coral reef — SNORKELERS love bobbing atop and observing action below — youngsters splash about the shallow swim pool. Remember, DON'T WALK ON REEF. Permanent damage will result. Car Parking for 200, Shower, Bathrooms, Boardwalk lifeguards.

STUART FL HUTCHINSON ISLAND (SOUTH TIP)   (561) 288-5690
A1A ST. LUCIE INLET (NORTH SIDE)   OPEN DAYLIGHT HOURS

BESTEST FUNNEST PORT

Exciting with lots going on — thats' PORT CANAVERAL! Deep water anchorage brings in the big bertha's. 70,000 tonners with 9 decks and 678 feet long... This is one of the *rare ports* "OPEN TO THE PUBLIC" Here's why I visit when I'm in the area. 3 Public parks - White Beach & Picnic Sites - Excellent Fishing Spots — 1.5 miles BIKING PATH — 5 Marinas & Seafood Eateries — 5 Public Boat Ramps — Jetty Park Campgrounds (35 Acres) plus ocean Splashing — LOCKS (good viewing) *Frequent Military & Historic Vessels Visit* — Many Festivals & Events On Weekends — I saw dolphin chugging along beside sleek luxury liners. The "PORT" is a grand place to spend the day!!

CAPE CANAVERAL, FL EAST END RD 528 ON KING BL   OPEN DAILY
PORT AUTHORITY (321) 783-7831   JETTY CAMPING (321) 783-7111

A "KINGLY" RESTORATION

The Spanish words "del rey" means *of the king* and at Delray Beach a truly royal effort has accomplished superior restorations of several DOWNTOWN HISTORIC DISTRICTS. Anchor site is Old School square (4 acres) with 1913 Elementary and 1925 High Schools. This is home To Cornell Museum having permanent exhibit of WORLD'S LARGEST COLLECTION OF MINIATURE SOLDIERS and many rotating displays...Surrounding (15 block) area contains MARINA HISTORIC

SECTION with buildings from 1922 in Mission, Monterey & Mediterranean styles. Area is near *drawbridge, faces Intracoastal Waterway* with scenic "Vet's Park" overlooking passing Mega-yachts! In NASSAU PARK DISTRICT (south of Atlantic Ave) you'll see 23 homes, 18 built between 1935 and 1941 of Cape Cod Revival type. DEL-IDA PARK RENOVATIONS include (many blocks) in Mediterranean style dating to 1923. I found the area especially charming because of the *botanicals in each small yard*— flaming poinsiannas, "grandpa Banyans" and huge-leafed Mangos! Do visit 1915 Cason Cottage (9 ft. ceilings) porte cochere and "ancient" switchboard...its twin is still used at the local Colony Hotel!!! ATLANTIC AVE. has wide promenades, tasty in & outdoor cafes and tranquil green pocket parks. Atlantic Ave. ends at (where else) n-a-t-c-h, the ATLANTIC OCEAN. Here are 3 miles of public beach beautified with Silver Eucalyptus, Gazebos and a wide promenade — bring your swim trunks!!!

DELRAY BEACH FL ATLANTIC AVE.
SWINTON AVE., LINTON BL N.E. 8TH ST.
N.E. 4TH ST., LAKE IDA RD
FEDERAL HWY & OCEAN BL (A1A)
CASON COTTAGE-5NE 1ST.   561-243-0223

OPEN DAILY
OLD SCHOOL SQUARE &
CORNELL MUSEUM
561-243-7922
OPEN TUES-SAT 11-4 SUN 1-4

MAKING A SPLASH

You can swim where the "champs" do! The INTERNATIONAL SWIMMING HALL OF FAME is open 365 days a year and is open to the public...just call ahead to make sure you don't get mixed up in a *"Butterfly Stroke" event!!!* The complex is spectacular having 3 pools & 2 of them are 50 meters by 25 yards. Dive well has 3 platform levels. Training pool holds 755,000 gallons. You may see Water Polo, Synchronized Swimming or pros on hi-dives. ISHOF is on a *peninsula* ringed by moorings where LUXURY YACHTS berth...On grounds is a 10,000 square foot MUSEUM. One of many, is the Johnny Weissmuller Exhibit — I saw every Tarzan movie ever made! Prestige events are held in a stadium seating 2,500!!!

FT. LAUDERDALE FL 501 SEABREEZE BL
OPEN 365 DAYS A YEAR

(954) 462-6536
ADMISSION

Tropical Islands

SHIPYARD ISLAND CAMPS — KAYAK TRAILS

Canoe paths are a maze beside scores of islands. Largest is Shipyard. It once had—homes groves & beach bridge. It is well treed & has 2 campsites. Primitive camping (13 sites) is on 11 ISLANDS, some are spoil islands beside I.C.W. The lagoon was home to Timucuan Indians. Prominent middens are Castle Windy & Turtle Mound. All SUMMER you see lots of (m & m's) manatee & mosquitos. Paddling twists about backwater flats having marvelous SPORTFISHING & "birding"!!! This destination is most popular with outdoor enthusiasts so 7 day advance permits are a must.

GRANT FARM ISLAND —
SPOIL ISLAND WITH A DIFFERENCE

The Indian River Aquatic Reserve is dotted with SPOIL ISLANDS, all *uninhabited* save one: GRANT FARM ISLAND. Accessible *only by boat,* this 800-foot long islet with its Australian pines and white beaches, is *paradise* to the 8 or 10 vacation homeowners whose houses are tucked here and there along the shore — each with its private dock! Those lucky folks don't have to look at the TUBE for entertainment! They can just *sit on their porches or docks* and watch a *constant parade* of passing BOATS — hundred-footers, paddlewheelers, canoes and all sizes in between!!! For this is the Intracoastal Waterway. Waters around Grant Farm Island offer *excellent crabbing, clamming, fishing* and (ahem) *"oystering."* Those folks must eat well!!!

GRANT, FL   FREE

ORCHID ISLAND

Oldtimers call it NORTH HUTCHINSON ISLAND! I call it *unusual because of its "low-key development"*. Homes are built behind dunes or below tree-top level!! Part of Orchids scenic beauty is a drive north through 7 miles of uninterrupted green...no development!! Suddenly, another surprise...to your west appear 2 miles of *meandering along coves and lagoons affording grand views.* I enjoyed a spectacular sunset!! Orchids best feature is its NUMEROUS BEACHFRONT PARKS. To name a few: Round Island, Vero, Jaycee, Conn, Humiston, Government Tracking and Wabasso. The frosting on this park system is 576-acre SEBASTIAN INLET STATE PARK on Orchid Island's north tip. Do visit or camp and *see why it's special!!!* Almost forgot...more fun is on orchids south tip at Ft. Pierce Recreation Area's 340-acre site.

NORTH BEACH CAUSEWAY, A1A — FT. PIERCE, FL
OPEN — DAILY   FREE

JACK ISLAND

Otters, marine animals and nesting birds cohabit on Jack's 958 acres. A FOOTBRIDGE spans lagoons leading to an OBSERVATION TOWER on Buttonwood Loop (1 mi.), Rabbit Run (2.2 mi.), or Trail Loop (2.1 mi.). The *plant and wildlife sanctuary shelters 119 bird types!!* Fishing is allowed either on the island or bridge. Jack Island's sister-park lies a stone's throw across Hwy. A1A. It is 32-acre PEPPER PARK on golden Atlantic shores, so hop on over for a dip!!

1 MI. NORTH ON A1A — FT. PIERCE INLET, FL
OPEN— DAILY   FREE

HUTCHINSON ISLAND

Nearly 50% of its 15-mile shoreline is set aside for PUBLIC USE. Atlantic surfside vistas begin on the island's north tip at JETTY PARK, then at every mile appear landscaped dune beach-parks!! Assuring JOHN Q. PUBLIC of his beach rights, 3 additional tracts have been added. They are GREEN TURTLE (323 acres); AVALON (398 acres) and BLIND CREED (431 acres). Touring this *idyllic 7-mile stretch,* views of Indian River coves invite you to pull over and soak up the scenery!! *June to August* residents roll out the red carpet for their beloved huge nesting SEA TURTLES. Eggs are incubated at the HOUSE OF REFUGE at island's south tip. Yes, they allow visitors (1-4 p.m. Tuesday thru Sunday). House of Refuge 1875 is only 1 of 9 remaining which gave aid to ship-wrecked sailors. *It perches on mammoth rocks* where 20 feet below Atlantic waves smash into crevices and pools creating new rock patterns. Camera shots are worth getting SEA SPRAYED!!! At Stuart Beach ELLIOT MUSEUM boasts a collection of 15 gorgeous vintage cars and lots more... Don't miss it! Hutchinson secrets more surprises on its green tropic shores...YOU'LL FIND THEM!!

2 MI. EAST ON A1A SEAWAY CAUSEWAY BRIDGE — FT. PIERCE, FL
OPEN — DAILY   FREE

MUNYON AND PEANUT ISLANDS

Dr. Munyon's famous "PAW-PAW ELIXER" and a *lavish hotel* brought worldwide travelers in 1900's. Its tropical 25 acres is accessible via a 10-min. trail walk (obstacle course), low trees and damp spots which ends at a sand spit where the remaining 50 feet of shallow water must be waded or tubed across depending on the tide!! Munyon is part of MacARTHUR BEACH STATE PARK. *Its 225 acres is the finest example* of Barrier Island Coastal Habitat remaining in Florida! PEANUT ISLAND is 2 miles south, cover 25 acres and is *accessible only by boat.* There is a Coast Guard Station and a bomb shelter built by the Kennedy's. A *strong current* surrounds Peanut's shores. Regular FERRY BOAT service!

MUNYON IS AT NORTH PALM BEACH, FL — WEST OF HWY. A1A
PEANUT IS AT RIVIERA BEACH, FL — EAST OF US1
OPEN— DAILY   FREE

DANIA BARRIER ISLAND

From tippy-top of New River Bridge you see the route of THE BARE-FOOT MAILMAN of 1880's. He walked this *same 11,500-foot beach stretch* which is now 244-acre JOHN U. LLOYD BEACH PARK!! Lloyd's 3 miles is home to NOVA MARINE RESEARCH and NAVY WEAPONS SYSTEMS. At the north end of *2 1/2 miles of gorgeous beachfront* are jetties for anglers and scuba diving for nearby offshore reefs. A curvy "leaning pine drive" crosses bridges leading to more activities than you have time for!!! Marina, docks and ramps give access to ICW if zooming up-n-down that waterway is your bag... Yup, CANOE RENTALS, TOO! "My druthers"?? Surf splashing near an "overloaded" picnic table! Outdoor buffs will want to explore marine life in THE TIDAL SOUND. Leave 45 minutes to stroll the SEMI-TROPICAL COASTAL HAMMOCK.

EAST ON A1A — DANIA, FL   (954) 923-2833
OPEN — DAILY   ADMISSION

DEERFIELD ISLAND PARK — A WELL-KEPT SECRET

Those who KNOW about it don't TALK about it, so many don't know it exists! But Deerfield Island Park is for *real!* This is the spot where AL CAPONE was supposed to have stashed his cache of bootleg!! More important, it's a *state refuge* for the GOPHER TORTOISE as well a home to GRAY FOX, RACCOONS, ARMADILLOS and SEA BIRDS! There's a *1500-foot boardwalk* MANGROVE TRAIL through over *8 acres* of RED, WHITE and BLACK MANGROVES — the *building blocks of island!!* The COQUINA TRAIL has a *lookout* over the Intracoastal! There's a picnic area, with tables and grills, a playground plus volleyball and horseshoes! Restrooms are nearby. NO FOOD CONCESSIONS, just a soda machine — *so brown-bag it.* The park is accessible only by BOAT. If you have your own, *there's a 10-slip marina for dockage.* Otherwise, FREE boat transportation is scheduled every Wed. and Sat. It leaves RIVERVIEW RESTAURANT dock 1741 Riverview Road at 8:30 a.m. Sullivan Park.

DIRECTIONS AS ABOVE — DEERFIELD BEACH, FL   (954) 360-1320
OPEN 8-5 DAILY   ADMISSION

Unique Shopping District

COCOA VILLAGE —

Cocoa — so named in 1880 after... what else but that *luscious beverage* which warmed our childhood tums! Right in the *heart* of this old Florida city is HISTORIC COCOA VILLAGE. Go sample the flavor of this *one-of-a kind village* as you stroll down tree-lined avenues and brick-paved streets. Here are shops and arcades, restaurants and bistros... *even a theater!!!* Watch as a potter turns a mound of clay into something PRETTY! Everywhere you'll see Old South, *turn-of-the century architecture,* gary striped awnings, balloons and oh, those tall *old oak trees* casting their *ample shade.* It's a trip into the *past,* but there's plenty of today and tomorrow to be seen. Plenty of parking, too. Before you depart, historic ST. MARK'S EPISCOPAL CHURCH, a few blocks away is well worth a visit as is the E.R. PORCHER HOUSE with its pillared facade.

THIS GRAND OLD LANDMARK IS OPEN FOR TOURS
KING ST. & BREVARD AVE. — COCOA, FL
OPEN — DAILY   FREE
PORCHER HOUSE   (407) 639-3500 ADMISSION

WORTH AVENUE — ULTIMATE IN SHOPPING

It simply OOZES *elegance!!!* This boulevard of shops and restaurants where the *rich and famous spend their money!!* And FAME isn't limited to the clientele! Oh, no, no, no! GUCCI, VAN CLEEF & ARPESL, BROOKS BROS., CHANEL, SAKS and SAINT LAURENT are just a few of the *illustrious names* which grace Worth Avenue!! It's said that this is one of THE most EXCLUSIVE shopping streets in the WORLD! Certainly it is PIC-TURESQUE with *Mediterranean-style* VILLAS, *wrought iron balconies, gay awnings* and *lush tropical greenery!* Don't miss THE ESPLANADE with its FOUNTAINS and beautiful GARDENS, home to some 48 BOU-TIQUES and SHOPS — even a BISTRO!! Valet parking, too. *Explore the charming sideways: VIA PARIGI, VIA ROMA, VIA DeMARIO and VIA MISNER... named for the famous ARCHITECT, ADDISON MISNER, who designed the 5-story VILLA you'll see there! Worth Avenue:* three blocks of SOMETHIN' ELSE!!!

WORTH AVENUE — PALM BEACH, FL   OPEN — DAILY   FREE

LAS OLAS — SHOPS AND CANALS

A sparkling dash of VENICE tucked away near a Spanish shopping quarter!! While foot and car bridges span secluded canals where INTER-NATIONAL YACHTSMEN outdo one another in the "grandeur" of their "floating palaces"!!! HUNDREDS OF VESSELS (bumper to bumper, stem to stern) line the waterways where their owners reside in *"posh canalside apartments."*When the Jet Setters get Ho- Hummed out with their floating routine they walk west on LAS OLAS BLVD. and "work out' with their cred-it cards. A median strip sports *tropical trees and bright posies* and brick crosswalks alternate with benches giving browsers rest opportunities. Persian rugs to royal gems...it can all be purchased on LAS OLAS. Don't expect shops to open early...Tut-Tut!! There are scrumptious places for lunch, you"ll find them! WINTER SEASON is best to get full flavor of Las Olas shop and canals district!!U.S.! I became quite *spoiled* at historic RIVERSIDE HOTEL.

LAS OLAS BLVD. — DOWNTOWN, FT. LAUDERDALE, FL   FREE
OPEN — DAILY RIVERSIDE HOTEL   (800) 325-3280 (954) 467-0671

OLDE NEW SMYRNA COMMERCIAL DISTRICT

Area covers about 10-12 blocks of "yesterdays downtown". In 1994 a renovation included a *"face lift and streetscape"* second to none! Decorative multicolored stone sidewalks runs the length of MAIN STREET (Canal St). which ends at the INDIAN RIVER where boats scur-ry to & fro! Just south is RIVERSIDE PARK and a bit north is OLD FORT PARK which contains historic Conner Free LIbrary. Canal street store-fronts house food emporiums plus every type specialty shops. The old town clock occupies a nich in a *green courtyard space* to watch passers-by. Some shop owners are descendants of Greeks and Minorcans who pioneered the area in 1760's!! There are frequent arts and craft festivals.

NEW SYMRNA FL CANAL ST.   C OF C (800) 541-9621
OPEN DAILY   FREE   OR (904) 428-2449

Animal Places

GATOR JUNGLE — A ROARING SUCCESS

If you're LUCKY you *might* hear an honest-to-gosh ROAR from some of the big BULL ALLIGATORS at GATOR JUNGLE in Christmas. Situated on Rd. 50, just 3 miles east of Christmas P.O., Gator Jungle has THOU-SANDS of these *prehistoric critters!!!* Plus a host of other wildlife: 'coons, coyotes, an African lion, monkeys, wild boar, turtles, exotic birds and a RARE FLORIDA PANTHER!! Things get *pretty exciting* every day at THREE when the gators and crocs are FED!!! This is a *breeding farm* as well as a tourist favorite. Gators are shipped to many places, 'specially *Israel* where GATOR TAIL is a *great delicacy.* Folks here in Florida kinda think so, too!

DIRECTIONS ABOVE — CHRISTMAS, FL (407) 568-2885
OPEN YEAR 'ROUND 9-6 ADMISSION

BREVARD ZOOLOGICAL PARK
FURRY FAUNA OF THE RARE & EXOTIC KIND

Ever see a PILEATED GIBBON? You'll see one name "CHOO-CHOO" at this sooper-dooper zoo!! He's *rare,* so take a good look! Meet "Buckles" the *African elephant,* and Herman, Florida's ONLY-FOR-SURE KODIAK BEAR!!! There are *jaguars, llamas, ostriches and 'gators; monkeys* — including a little SPIDER MONKEY — and o-mi-gosh, so many more crit-ters and birds. There;s food to be had for feeding the furries and a shad-ed PICNIC AREA for feeding yourselves. It's just a GREAT place for fam-ily FUN!!!

MELBOURNE, FL EAST OF I-95 WICKHAM RD. (321) 254-9453
OPEN 10-5 DAILY ADMISSION

DREHER PARK ZOO

What's a vacation without a trip to the ZOO?!!! Got to have a look at all the animals. And at DREHER PARK you'll see a bunch of 'em!! Wander through this *20-acre furry farm* filled with lush gardens and over 60 SPECIES of *domestic and exotic animals.* TINY MARMOSETS — *rare and endangered* are they ... OCELOTS, GIANT ALDABRA TORTOISE, DIANA MONKEYS, REPTILES and *bee-u-tiful* BIRDS! *Cuddle baby ani-mals* at the PETTING ZOO or stroll down the *Betty Cardinal Nature Trial* with its exotic plant life. Picnic tables and light refreshments are to be had and if you arrange it in advance, you can even celebrate a BIRTHDAY with a PARTY AT THE ZOO!!! *The kids will love it!*

1301 SUMMIT BLVD. — WEST PALM BEACH, FL (561) 533-0887
OPEN — DAILY 9A.M.-5 P.M. ADMISSION

LION COUNTRY SAFARI

You don't have to go to AFRICA for this one! But you'll think you're there as you drive 8 miles of Safari Trail through country that looks like the AFRICAN VELDT!!! Everywhere you look you'll see *lions,* of course, plus zebras, giraffes, rhinos, chimps, all kinds of antelope AND ELEPHANTS! *Keep your car windows closed* because there guys aren't behind bars! They roam FREE in the 640-acre game preserve. No convertibles allowed, folks, but rental cars are available. So are rides on friendly ele-phants or a cruise on Lake Shanalee aboard the SAFARI QUEEN. Treat the "Hungries" to a bite at the park restaurant, play miniature golf or visit THE REPTILE CENTER! It's a *neat* place for a family outing and A MUST for visitors!!!

SOUTHERN BLVD. — WEST PALM BEACH, FL (10 MILES WEST)
OPEN — DAILY, RAIN OR SHINE, 9:30 A.M.-4:30 P.M.   (561) 793-1084
STATE RD 80   ADMISSION

GATORAMA

Gator farming is different than tomato farming — here's why. Some are 16 feet long. Population is 2000 gators, 1000 hatchlings and 250 crocs! An enclosed lake walkover gets you almost "nose to nose" with these prehistoric critters. You may feed them and *when they spy that food bag — they "come a -flyin'"* GATORAMA is a commercial MEAT AND HIDES FARM tightly controlled by the state. Over 6 tons of chicken and barrels of fish make the weekly diet. The grow-out house (Alligator Condo) is for the wee ones. Larger guys (2-4 feet) are in tiled pens and like to *stack themselves like pancakes* to bask in the sun! One huge gator is "spoon-fed" as he is injured. Here's the method. They tap his snout gently and if he is hungry he opens up and they "shovel in" his special formula! Gator meat is shipped all over the world (Europe, japan and fast catching on in the U.S. of A.). Patty's GATOR GRILL serves samples and you may also buy to take home!!

HWY. 27 — SOUTH OF PALMDALE, FL   (863) 675-0623
OPEN — DAILY SUNUP-SUNDOWN   ADMISSION

JOHN D. EASTERLIN PARK — TRANQUIL OASIS

Ever PAT A PEACOCK?! Here's your chance!! Easterlin Park has a bunch of 'em!!! This is a *favorite spot for residents and visitors alike.* Some 50 acres of CYPRESS, MIXED CYPRESS FOREST, WILD COFFEE DAHOON HOLLY, FERNS — even RED MAPLES abound!! There are 3 SHADED *picnic areas,* a children's *playground* and 55 RENTAL CAMPSITES!! A 3/4 mile long NATURE TRAIL winds through OAK HAMMOCK, CYPRESS and MAPLE! Thing to do? How about HORSESHOES, VOLLEYBALL and SHUFFLEBOARD!! There's even a FITTNESS COURSE for adults! Easterlin is located just off I-95, but once you're in the park, you wouldn't think there was a highway nearby!

100 N.W. 38TH ST. — OAKLAND PARK, FL   (954) 938-0610
OPEN — DAILY   ADMISSION

REAL HAMS

Hard to tell who enjoys Miami SEAQUARIUM most, the sea creature performers or the squealing audience!! On 35 acres you meet Lolita (whale), Salty (Sea Lion) and notorious Flipper (T.V. Star). 1990's have been a *baby booming era* for dolphin;, sea lion and Juliet with other manatee producing 13 "mini" manatees! BABY FEEDING TIME is a *star attraction* at Seaquarium! Other exhibits are SHARK FEEDING TANKS, sea turtle and neon fish aquariums, flamingos and rare birds... I learned much in 4 of their many displays...LOST ISLAND WILDLIFE HABITAT, FACES OF RAINFORESTS, LIFE EDGE TOUCH POOL, and WATER-

WINGS STINGRAY POOL. *Additional (40) aquariums* are awesome —
One word of caution — When 9,000 pound Lolita leaps 20 feet in the air,
L-O-O-K O-U-T!!!

4400 Rickenbacker Causeway — Key Biscayne, FL   (305) 361-5705
Open — Daily 9:30-6:30   Admission

FLOATING PIGGIE BLOBS

Only camels look more weird! Manatee resemble a gigantic floating
scoop of lard with a piglet snout on one end and a flat "pizza paddle" on
the other. Manatee ogling is the #1 activity in HISTORIC MELBOURNE
VILLAGE... From the banks of *Crane Creek Park* I saw about 30 (babies)
too. A neat promenade, 10-ft-wide boardwalk, tall green trees, decorative
night lights and benches makes this a "beauty spot". Wildlife display
cases catch your eye as will the MANATEE SCULPTURE in adjacent
Holmes Park...Manatee Facts... Length-13 ft., Weight-3,000 lbs., Food-
Aquatic plants & can eat 15% of body weight daily. Gestation for "baby
blobs"-13 months, Communication-Squeaks & squeals.

Melbourne Fl Melbourne Ave. C of C   (321) 724-5400
between US 1 bridge & railroad bridge
Crane Creek Promenade   Open Daily-7 Days   FREE

Inlet Adventures

WHERE SEA MEETS RIVER 8 COASTAL INLETS

The ultimate inexpensive (CHEAP) lollygagging DAYTRIP is a visit to
any *"inlets"* listed below... keyword at ALL INLETS is A-C-T-I-O-N! Not
wishing to overexert myself I usually take a cooler, plunk down in a lawn
chair and prepare to watch the *"drama of human events"* unfold — my
absolute best belly laughs have been during my inlet watches!!

SEBASTIAN INLET — A mix of wild water & *unpredictable Captains.*•
576 Acre State Park • Longest Bridge Span • Jetties • 3 Mile Swim Beach
• Scuba Drive

Sebastian Fl Brevard & Indian River Counties Hwy A1A   (561) 984-4852

FT PIERCE INLET — Jetties (north & south) • S. Jetty topped by *sidewalk*
• 340 Acre park (north) • Surfing • Heavy Boat Use • Picnic Park (s. side) •
Swimming • Lots Bistros (S. Side) • Motels ON Inlet • Coast Guard Station

Ft. Pierce Fl North & South Causeways   Hwy A1A

ST. LUCIE INLET — Indian River, St. Lucie River & Atlantic Converge •
Jetties • 928 Acre State Park (north Jupiter Island) • Sea Turtle Nesting
May-August • *Bathtub Beach* Reef Park Swimming.

ST. LUCIE INLET STATE REEF PARK — Submerged lands 1.4 mi. by
4.7 mil (5-35 ft) • *Good Diving & Snorkeling* • (561) 744-7603 • INLET

ACCESS (BOAT ONLY) or BEACH-WALK from Bath-Tub Beach

STUART FL S. HUTCHINSON ISLAND HWY A1A MARTIN CO PARKS (561) 288-5690

JUPITER INLET — Lighthouse (tours) (561) 747-6639 • Jetties • Dubois Park (30 acres) Beach & *Pioneer Home on Indian Midden* (tours) (561) 747-6639 • Jupiter Beach Park (47 Acres) Oceanfront: Complete Facilities • fishing • 3.5 Mile Scenic Drive (S. A1A) *Oceanfront*-Carlin Dune Restoration Area.

JUPITER FL SOUTH SIDE LOXAHATCHEE RIVER US 1 TO OCEAN BL (A1A) TO JUPITER BEACH RD.   OPEN DAILY COUNTY PARKS DEPT. (561) 966-6600

BOYNTON INLET — I really like this inlet. You can almost *"touch"* the boats as they bob in & out the pass!!! • Jetties • 8 Acre Ocean Inlet Park (Inland Side) • Marina • Eating Spots • Seawall Fishing • Swimsuits (gals & guys) run the g-a-m-u-t...Bring the camcorder!!

NEAR BOYNTON BEACH AT OCEAN RIDGE FL   (561) 966-6600
6990 N. OCEAN BL (A1A)   OPEN DAILY

BOCA RATON INLET — Super Entertaining • Luxury, Yachts • Overlooks huge "Lake Boca Raton" • Constant bridge raising • Jetties • 11 Acre South Inlet Park (Scenic) I often stay at the "gracious" *tropical* BRIDGE HOTEL (on the inlet, on the lake) & oceanviews. They've a *waterside cafe* for super food plus views of water sports activity in the "pass"! Crowning the 11 story hotel is an *elegant rooftop restaurant...* More unusual is hotel parking grounds (a mini-botanical garden) Bring B-I-K-E-S...lovely cycling!!

BOCA RATON FL 1298 S. OCEAN BL (A1A)   OPEN DAILY
SOUTH INLET PARK   ADMISSION
BRIDGE HOTEL 999 E. CAMINO REAL
800-327-0130 OR (561) 368-9500

PORT EVERGLADES INLET
Where the big boys berth (1,500 ocean liners) dock at PORT EVER-GLADES • 10 & 12 deckers sail the "pass • Viewing from *John U.Lloyd State Park* (244 Acres) • 2.5 mi beach • Jetties • Fishing • Canoe Rentals

FT. LAUDERDALE, DANIA FL   DANIA BEACH BL TO OCEAN DR.

JOHN U. LLOYD STATE PARK   OPEN DAILY   (954) 923-2833
LAKE WORTH INLET - POWER PLANT MANATEES

LAKE WORTH INLET POWER PLANT MANATEES — Since 1946 tubby MANATEES have flocked to riviera Power Plant canal. The "frigid" winter of 2001 I saw 75 big guys bobbing about here!! Viewing is excellent....A small museum is on grounds. I admired (outdoor) manatee paintings on a l-o-o-o-g wall.

WEST PALM BCH, FL — FPL RIVIERA POWER PLANT AT 59TH ST &
POINSETTIA AVE — OPEN JAN & FEB 8 AM - 3 PM   (800) 552-8440

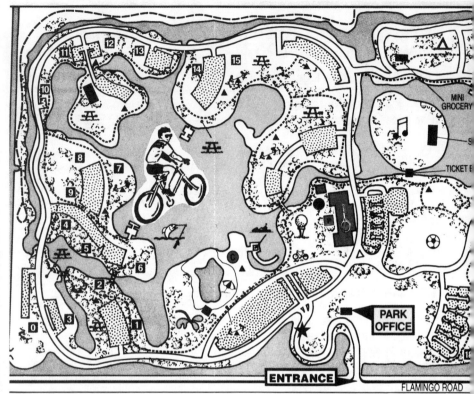

★ **GATE HOUSE** - Entrance fee weekends/holidays. SEE PG. 22

PARK OFFICE **PARK OFFICE** - For information, shelter reservations, sports and game bag rentals, etc.

 BEACH FACILITIES - Swimming, beach, bath house, children's playground, rest rooms. Entrance fee (children three and under free with parent.)

 WATERSLIDE/TUBE RIDE - 700 foot waterslide, 400 foot tube ride. Call for fees, rules and regulations.

 TENNIS/RACQUETBALL CENTER - Ten lighted hard tennis courts, six lighted three-wall racquetball courts. Pro-shop. Membership and hourly rates. Call for reservations, fees, hours, lessons, etc.

 MINIATURE GOLF - 18-hole course. Fee.

 BOAT RENTALS - Canoe, paddleboat, kayak and aquacycle rentals. Fee and deposit. Children under 14 must be accompanied by an adult.

 BIKING/JOGGING PATH 5.7 MI.

 EQUESTRIAN TRAIL

C. B. SMITH PARK
BIKING

⛺ **LAKESIDE CAMPGROUND** - Sixty R.V. sites with full hook-ups and eleven tent sites. Showers, rest rooms, laundry, and mini-grocery. Reservations suggested. Fee.

1 **PICNIC SHELTERS** - Four extra large (160+ capacity), six large (80+ capacity), and eight medium (50+ capacity). All with grills, water, tables, and electricity. Reservation fee and deposit.

P **PAVILION PICNIC AREA** - Large picnic shelter and picnic area for groups of 300 or more with a variety of amenities.

🏕 **PICNIC AREAS** - Tables/grills throughout the park on a first come basis.

C **CONCESSION** - At swimming beach. Food, beverages, picnic supplies. Open year-round.

🚲 **BICYCLE RENTALS** - Single, and tandem, some with baby seat. Fee and deposit.

🐟 **FISHING** - Permitted (shore, pier, and boat) except in Marina area. Catch and release encouraged.

-58-

LAKE OSBORNE CYCLING

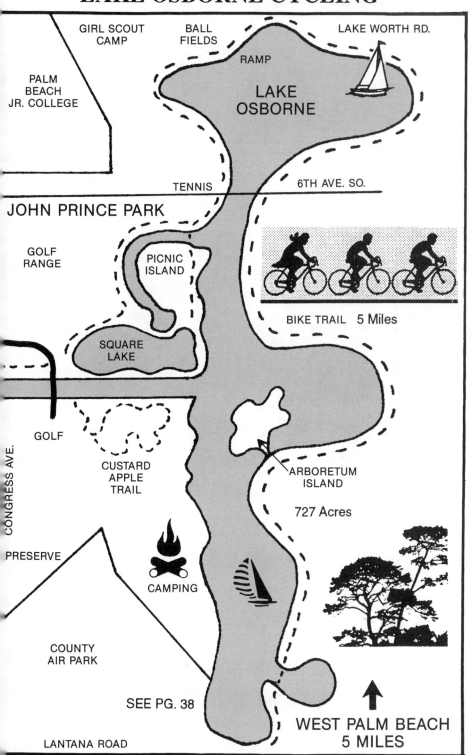

GIRL SCOUT CAMP

BALL FIELDS

LAKE WORTH RD.

RAMP

PALM BEACH JR. COLLEGE

LAKE OSBORNE

TENNIS

6TH AVE. SO.

JOHN PRINCE PARK

GOLF RANGE

PICNIC ISLAND

BIKE TRAIL   5 Miles

SQUARE LAKE

CONGRESS AVE.

GOLF

CUSTARD APPLE TRAIL

ARBORETUM ISLAND

727 Acres

PRESERVE

CAMPING

COUNTY AIR PARK

SEE PG. 38

WEST PALM BEACH 5 MILES

LANTANA ROAD

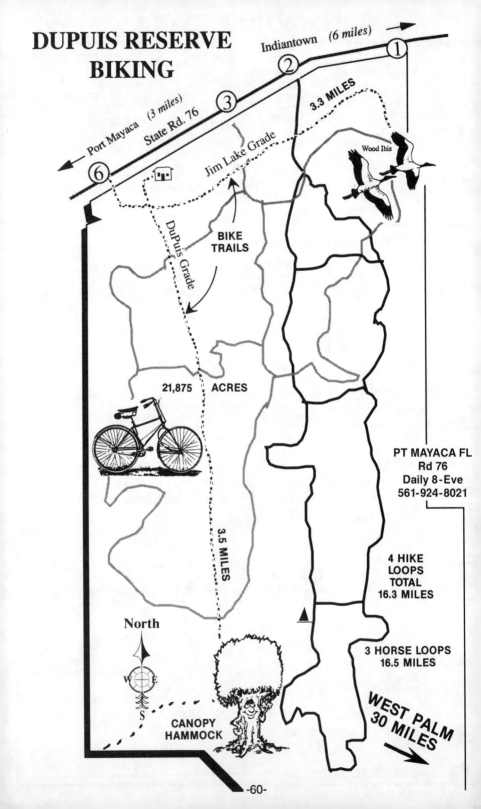

DUPUIS RESERVE
BIKING

Indiantown *(6 miles)*

①

②

Port Mayaca *(3 miles)*

State Rd. 76

③

3.3 MILES

Jim Lake Grade

Wood Ibis

⑥

BIKE TRAILS

DuPuis Grade

21,875 ACRES

PT MAYACA FL
Rd 76
Daily 8-Eve
561-924-8021

3.5 MILES

4 HIKE
LOOPS
TOTAL
16.3 MILES

3 HORSE LOOPS
16.5 MILES

North

W — E
S

WEST PALM
30 MILES

CANOPY
HAMMOCK

BRIAN PICCOLO PARK

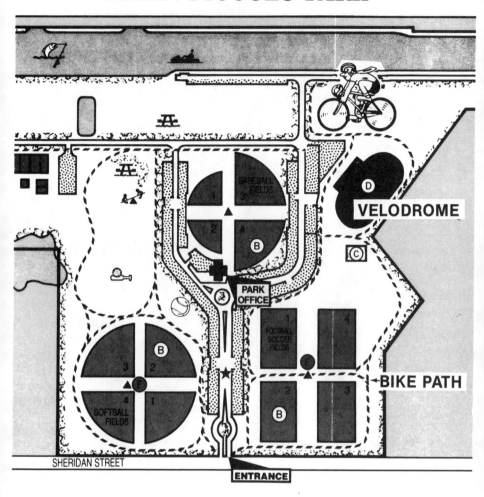

Legend

 VELODROME - Two sloped recreational and competitive tracks — an outer track 333.3 meters long and an inner track 198 meters long.

 HOME RUN BATTING CAGES - Seven stations for softball and/or baseball. Fee. Call 433-2727 for information.

 BOAT RENTALS - Paddle boat and canoe rentals at Park office. Boat pickup and launch area at the lake on the north side of the park.

 FISHING - Permitted. Catch and release encouraged.

 PICNIC AREAS - Tables/grills available on a first-come basis.

 PLAYGROUND

 FOOD CONCESSION

 **JOGGING/BIKE PATH**

▲ **REST ROOMS**

ROLLER SKATING

 COOPER CITY FL
9501 Sheridan St
Daily
954-437-2600

MacARTHUR BEACH STATE PARK

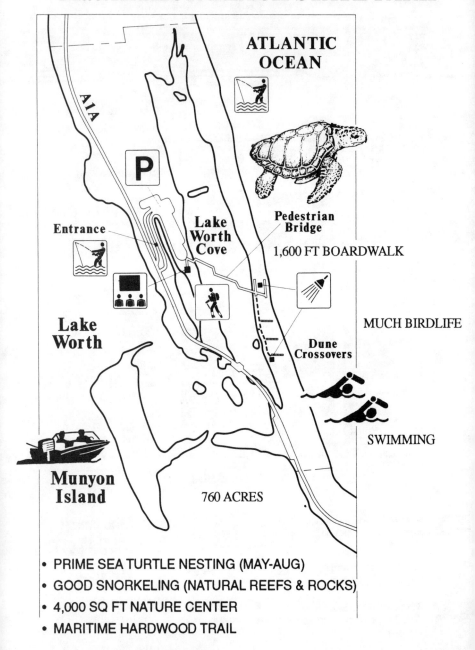

ATLANTIC OCEAN

P

Entrance

Lake Worth Cove

Pedestrian Bridge

1,600 FT BOARDWALK

MUCH BIRDLIFE

Lake Worth

Dune Crossovers

SWIMMING

Munyon Island

760 ACRES

A1A

- PRIME SEA TURTLE NESTING (MAY-AUG)
- GOOD SNORKELING (NATURAL REEFS & ROCKS)
- 4,000 SQ FT NATURE CENTER
- MARITIME HARDWOOD TRAIL

NORTH PALM BEACH FL HWY A1A   (561) 624-6950
OPEN DAILY   NATURE CENTER   (561) 624-6952

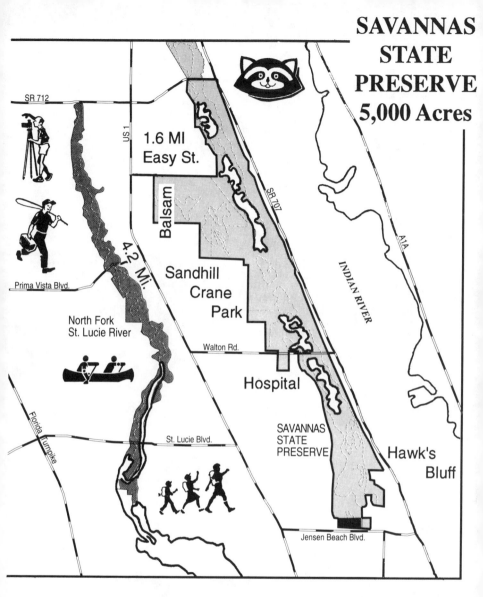

A rare 10 mi. long 5,000 acre web of 6 biological communities. COASTAL BLUFFS mix with marshes & pine flats. Nature Study, Canoeing, Hiking & Fishing are popular....Preserve has excellent. WILDLIFE! Hike Entrances (north) off Balsam St. also (east) at Sandhill Crane Park (off Walton Rd). For south entrance go east on Jensen Bch. Bl. to Savanna Rd. north to gate 13. CANOE LAUNCH is .4 mi. south of Walton Rd. Go to deadend on Riverview, go to Gumbo Limbo Ln. (small put-in).

JENSEN BEACH FL   CANOE TOURS D E P (561) 468-3985
OPEN DAILY 8-SUNSET   (561) 340-7530

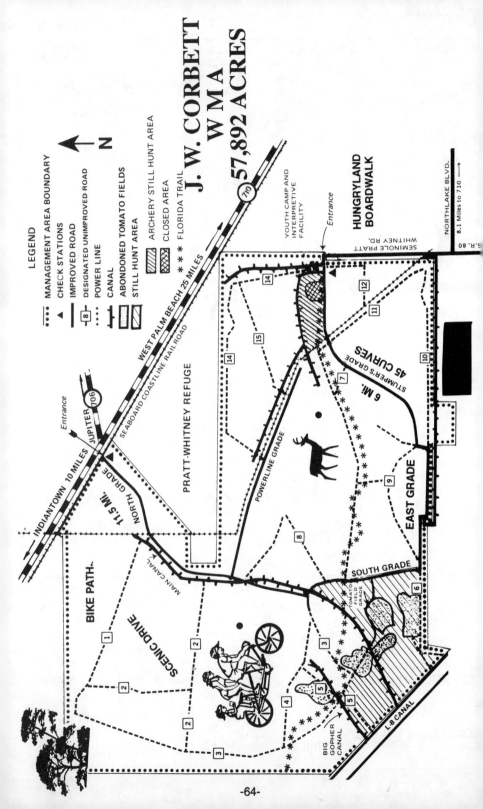

J. W. CORBETT WMA
57,892 ACRES

LEGEND

- ●●● MANAGEMENT AREA BOUNDARY
- ▲ CHECK STATIONS
- ●● IMPROVED ROAD
- 8 DESIGNATED UNIMPROVED ROAD
- POWER LINE
- ●●● CANAL
- STILL HUNT AREA
- ▨ ARCHERY STILL HUNT AREA
- ▩ CLOSED AREA
- ∗∗∗ FLORIDA TRAIL
- ▨ ABONDONED TOMATO FIELDS

N

710

INDIANTOWN 10 MILES
JUPITER 706
Entrance

WEST PALM BEACH 25 MILES

SEABOARD COASTLINE RAIL ROAD

PRATT-WHITNEY REFUGE

NORTH GRADE
11.5 MI.

MAIN CANAL

BIKE PATH
SCENIC DRIVE

POWERLINE GRADE

STUMPER'S GRADE
45 CURVES
6 MI.

YOUTH CAMP AND INTERPRETIVE FACILITY

Entrance

HUNGRYLAND BOARDWALK

SEMINOLE PRATT WHITNEY RD.

EAST GRADE

SOUTH GRADE

TOMATO FIELD GRADE

BIG GOPHER CANAL

L-8 CANAL

NORTHLAKE BLVD.
8.1 Miles to 710
S.R. 80

14 15 14 7 9 8 12 11 10 6 5 4 3 2 1

-64-